LAUNDRY LINES

Published in Canada by
Inanna Publications and Education Inc.
210 Founders College, York University
4700 Keele Street, Toronto, Ontario M3J 1P3
Telephone: (416) 736-5356 Fax (416) 736-5765
Email: inanna.publications@inanna.ca Website: www.inanna.ca

We gratefully acknowledge the support of the Canada Council for the Arts and
the Ontario Arts Council for our publishing program. We also acknowledge
the financial support of the Government of Canada through the Canada Book
Fund.

Original cover concept: Emily Wood
Final cover design: Val Fullard

Library and Archives Canada Cataloguing in Publication

Carson, Ann Elizabeth, 1929-, author
        Laundry lines : a memoir in stories and poems / Ann Elizabeth Carson.

(Inanna memoir series)
Issued in print and electronic formats.
ISBN 978-1-77133-269-9 (paperback). – ISBN 978-1-77133-270-5 (epub). –
ISBN 978-1-77133-272-9 (pdf)

        1. Carson, Ann Elizabeth, 1929-. 2. Carson, Ann Elizabeth, 1929-
–Family. 3. Feminists--Canada--Biography. 4. Poets, Canadian (English)–21st
century–Biography. 5. Psychotherapists–Canada–Biography. 6. Toronto
(Ont.)–Biography. I. Title.

PS8605.A85Z53 2015   C811'.6   C2015-905005-7
                                             C2015-905006-5

Printed and Bound in Canada.

MIX
Paper from
responsible sources
FSC® C004071

LAUNDRY LINES

A Memoir in
Stories and Poems

ANN ELIZABETH CARSON

INANNA
Memoir Series

To four sisters, Aunts Damaris, Gertrude, Helen
and my mother Grace—my loving foundation,
and for Michael, who lit the fire and helped keep it burning.

Table of Contents

But bringing to speech part of one's self that has had reason to keep silent is frightening, painful, and even dangerous.

—Jeanne Perreault

If you end your story it's a static work of art, a finite circle. But if you don't, it belongs to anyone's imagination. It stays alive forever.

—Jodi Picoult

Poetry ... illuminates, touches down, and continues along filaments and in bright spots or curves around us, or comes in the back door. Poetry is a way to describe and distill, but remain porous, oxygenated. Poetry lets the light in.

— Kelley Aitken

Marilyn Walsh, "Diving," Wings and Wires series, 2008, Mixed media,
etchings with embroidery, 6 x 4 inches.

Introduction

"WHY WOULD I, AN AVOWED FEMINIST, ACTIVIST AND AUTHOR, select *Laundry Lines* as a title for my fifth book?" That's what my friends and family asked me. Laundry? With all its cultural connotations as women's usually unpaid or low-waged work? Lines of laundry, on screeching backyard wires strung between poles and trees, a woman bending and stretching as she pins up the wash. Yes, but pleasant images, too—sun and warmth and breeze and flapping sounds, a more natural way of living. All true. But for me, there's much more to it than that. *Laundry Lines* is a metaphor for the stories we remember, the tales we select from our past and hang on the line: hung out to dry for all to see and examine.

Laundry Lines: A Memoir in Stories and Poems is about the imperative to tell our stories for our individual and collective survival. The complex emotional inheritance and painful undertow in families unfolds. Gradually we see the slow reconciliation with the blows and beauties meted out by life that comes with age, and the healing power of the deep sensual salve offered by surrender to nature.

Laundry Lines weaves together poetry and prose, uncovering fine gradations of meaning in family stories and in storytelling itself. At 86, I have a long view of the effect on the psyche of war, economic recession, loss, forgiveness, family myths and inheritance, and much else. As a psychotherapist and artist familiar with Jung and the power of myth, I try in these pages to shed light on current struggles by mapping myths and archetypes over our familiar stories.

These stories and poems look to the past from the perspective of a contemporary (white, middle-class) feminist. They are inevitably defined by this particular perspective. As you wander through the pages, you may glean how Canadian lives were shaped by the Depression, World War Two, and subsequent changes in social policy. An evocation of my aunts and their home in Cheltenham, Ontario, for instance, reveals the rich and powerful ground for my emerging sense of self as I listened to their conversations with some of Canada's pioneering feminist activists, including Charlotte Whitton and Dr. Marion Hilliard. The former served as the first female mayor of a major Canadian city (Ottawa) and was instrumental in shifting the country away from the institutionalization of parentless children into a foster care system, Hilliard wrote groundbreaking articles about women's health for *Chatelaine* magazine, published *A Woman Doctor Looks at Love and Life, Women and Fatigue* (still in print today) and led the drive for the creation of Women's College Hospital in Toronto. What better way to launch into life than with the intellectual and emotional shaping of these strong, intelligent women.

The title of this book is taken from a poetic exploration of similarities between the coded language used by women and by those working on the Underground Railway. For instance, the positioning of laundry on a line could tell an "unspeakable" family story to neighbourhood housewives. And particular quilted patterns were used to convey whether a travel route was safe for escaping slaves. I draw on my experience as a psychotherapist and writer to explore the role of women's hidden language and how we communicate a rich subterranean world of emotion and knowledge subtly to one another, in the same way that quilted shapes hung along roadways were a wordless language that helped black slaves escape to Canada.

Always, there is the theme of needed connection through stressful times. Whatever the cause of grief—casualties of war or weather or a brutal economic system—"each of us has a long history of strength and endurance, and now, the tension and mystery of balancing old and new ways of resourcefulness so that we can survive." I try to overlay personal struggles with planetary ones, drawing analogies between the two, again using insights learned over decades of practice as a psychotherapist.

Many poems and stories in the book reflect the profound healing we can find in nature. I feel we must draw deeply from this well as we wrestle on a planetary level and personally with how to pull back from the brink of extinction in an age of climate change and dying oceans ... the life-support system of the Earth. Taking the global struggle to a personal level is relevant to anyone who cares about the fate of our home. We all need help untangling the strands that make up our psyches, and so too the collective fabric we all weave on a political and public level.

Perhaps you will hang out some of your own laundry one day. May you find in these poetic and prose reflections on issues great and small some insights gathered from an elder feminist, environmental and social justice advocate, mother, colleague and friend.

DETAIL OF SECTIONS

"Laundry Lines: Prospects and Constraints" is about the urgency of stories, the shaping of childhood experience and an early bonding with nature. "Border Lines: Loss and Redemption" consists of tales of adolescence and war, of desolation and forgiveness. There is a much longer story, not written here, of my involvement in feminism. Reading Betty Friedan "woke me up," postgraduate studies showed me how various feminist critiques have shaped and contributed to worldwide thought and action on inequality, race, poverty, and climate change. The four poems in "Border Lines," I hope, at least encapsulate that adventure.

Throughout a sometimes stormy life and an often loner existence, I have remained an optimist. As an urban and academic woman, I strive for balance by tapping into the sustaining power of love of family and of nature, as I envision it in "Life Lines: Nature's Lineage." As Marion Woodman has often said, the still point is all the more precious for our not often reaching it.

Life Laundry
Prospects and Constraints

Marilyn Walsh, "Great Expectations," Wings and Wires series, 2008, Mixed media, etchings with embroidery, 4 x 6 inches.

We Must Tell Our Stories

We are born into a story. Layered threads woven deep
trail tracks on maps unread.
We gaze in wonder at what we are supposed to know.

We sleep through symbols, reluctant, yet challenged
to make them our own, grappling with what to keep,
or give away, as we meet our birthed-in story

always behind us, never forgotten. Earth-bound,
hidden or rearing up as needed, unforeseen,
while we gaze in wonder as what we are supposed to know

beckons — a hybrid flower opening to thick-fibred centuries,
threads of always has been, and a ready cache of seed
as we gaze in wonder at what we are supposed to know

about other stories yeasting; muffled murmurings
through time invite belief, disclose how differences leak
the story that gives us birth, may push us   to speak

before the light goes out. Or else rejoin the motherlode
unknown. Listen. Hear the faint, waiting hums that heed
disembodied stories strung juicy deep, ours to be born into
when we gaze in wonder at the little we have come to know.

Laundry Life

Monday morning coffee smells and pulley squeaks
as my mother hangs clothes on two steel lines,
strung garden-length;
wooden pegs in a pouch on the line, the next peg
in her mouth — she could even talk around it.
First pinned are sheets and towels, then pants and skirts
pulled out to dangle over the tomato plants
at the back of the yard.

Shirts and blouses next, collars down
so shoulders dry without a mark. Underwear,
never bras, hang close to the house, almost hidden
behind the vine-covered breakfast room wall.
Socks line up just so, toes point in one direction
The days the heels and toes face each
other is a sure sign of trouble brewing.

Rainy day lines criss-cross the open basement beams
over a hand-cranked mangle, steamy laundry tubs
and perspiring, never sweaty, mothers.
We kids peer in the neighbour's window
to an identical scene, rest chins on the sill at driveway level,
yellow boots and knobby knees leave dry patches
on the pavement, along with the news from our side

kids were out in all weather
as long as they were together

Sheets hang blinding white in sunny winter rows,
dry stiff as boards, crack down the middle in a perfect
fold. My sister and I snicker
at the ossified pajama legs and other unseemly juttings.
We carry them under our arms into the house
to thaw over radiators.
The smell of frost and sunshine lingers
as they droop to the floor.

Waitressing to earn my university fees
between meals, I help the laundress string
long rows of flopping sheets
behind Monhegan's Island Inn. Out of sight
of strolling guests the ropes stretch — salt would rust metal.
Long beach towels brush the grass,
their coloured curves, white fringed borders mirror
ocean waves that glint and foam along the shore.
I beg a corner of the line for uniforms, socks and "smalls"
hard to dry in my small dorm room.

Newly wed, our below-ground city apartment
boasts no green or cellar spaces. A tangle of ropes
stretched on a wooden frame in the bathtub
behind closed doors collapses without warning
under the weight of dripping hand-wrung garments.
Celebrating our eagerly awaited intimacy and freedom,
who cares? Until the baby came. I learned to drive

an old English mini, baby buckled in beside laundry
heaped high in the back seat.
I rattle up Spadina's red cobbles to new machines
beside my mother's basement laundry tubs.
Wash three loads, hang out, take in, hang out,

fold and fold and fold, catch up on family news,
neighbourhood gossip. Grandma and baby play,
cook a second-helping-of-meat dinner. Good trade.

A new baby on the way. We look
for a new home where children can play

and parents claim a toy-free corner. Find a hot little
house down-payment-boosted from parental pockets.
A big garden backs onto a stream for now,
suburban women chat across fences, laundry placed
neat on "roundabouts."
Plastic lines in four-square metal frames,
placed carefully for the wind to find drying room,
quiver with diapers, sleepers two sizes now,
man shirts collars down in every straight-edged garden.

Always I write. Words are in spaces
between soak and churn, laundry, tears
laughter and weary bones, between
hang out in every weather. Places found
to dry, fold and sort once more in
the stream of family gatherings, the allure
of new friends and blossoming career.

Back to the city. I said it was more children
a third is imminent but no libraries or book stores,
no trees or art galleries, drove me crazy.
A creaky old house on a shady curved street. A washer
and dryer. No clothes shall hang below in the basement,
no roundabouts allowed in city gardens. We work
behind shiny painted doors. I never liked the neighbourhood.
No children peered in the windows.

The relief of Haliburton summers! Ropes strung on branches
between trees, sag under bathing suits, towels speckled with pollen,

insects fly into them, snagged unawares in the dappled sun.
We travel through two lakes and up the river to town
in the big dory once a week.
Sheets, machine-dried while we shop, are piled
beside bulging bags as four small chins drip ice cream
down their shirts. Lake smells
scent the beds for a night or two.

A marriage behind me with 22 years to sort:
what to keep, what else to leave behind? Move on
to a small detached, a friendly front verandah,
with two steel lines strung garden length from porch
to fence

       by John, the youngest one,
       the other children on their own. I dream

new gardens, hang a weekly laundry
with plastic pegs from the pouch on the line,
talk around the one in my mouth as new neighbours
air the week's news.

Children grown — a stacked town-house,
a stacked washer/dryer in a cupboard,
the shower rod my laundry line for "hang to dry."
Socks droop over water heater pipes,
sweaters on a towel drape over the toilet seat,
or lie flat in the bathtub.

On a good day
clothes dangle over chairs and plastic-covered metal rods,
the old wood drying rack re-incarnated, out of sight
behind the gate and the climbing hydrangea
in my patio haven. Until
John's spring-time death. Scoured to the marrow, stripped
root and branch, flesh folds carefully over fragile bone.

No gardens.
No life-line
anywhere spreads everywhere endlessly ahead.

I take refuge
in the land and lakes of *The Manitoulin,*
stretch out on grass, rock or dock. Floating on the water
suspended between earth and sky, I watch a contrail
cleave the entrails of gunpowder clouds.

What origin propels? What path re-orients a destination?
When the light has changed colour, the horizon
disappeared and the world is unrecognizable.
I write to hear my heart, to feel my breath
salvage body and mind
  unearth roots
  redeem passion

Mind Cellar

Memories lived and memories learned
good and bad reside together
not apart, as some insist.

They stand alone and side
by side.
Jewelled jars for every season
preserved on mind-shelves, waiting.

The deeper missing is for the lost ones
unshelved. Aliveness will be in each,
in the other and together.

Just as peace is in forgiving, while
not forgetting to remember
that learning to live
is day by day

and that it's been okay.

The Play

Her stage. Her act. Who writes
the play? Who composes the music?
Bone-bred, muscle molding,
stomach holding heritage.

Not just a paper chart, lines
descendant sprouting arms with notes:
Birth, Marriage, Death — a genealogy
alive on faces in a family album.

A longing look reveals their heart heavy
singing, brain-wracked birthright.
The same smiles come from behind
to stretch ahead forever.

Their charted stage is mine, acts
frozen on a page write today's play,
makes the music that pulls
sound and fury from age-old silences.

Easy to say take a break — to look for colour
outside the lines, sniff a sprig of dill,

cherished memory on my windowsill.
And when I savour tongue-tingly rhubarb pie,

make unrhymed poems, answer
city-bird calls and foghorns in daylight.
I paddle the moon path, risking a tomorrow
without answers.

Weave and Mend[1]

MY LAST VISIT WITH GERTRUDE IS AT BELMONT HOUSE IN JUNE of 1994 just before I leave for Manitoulin Island for the summer. For the first time she is lying in bed in daytime, head propped on pillows, and I know she has finally surrendered. While she always seems glad to see me when I visit, she hasn't known my name for a year, knows I am familiar, but not who I am. She calls out "Oh oh oh" on and on, stops for a while when I squeeze her hand, stroke her arm or cheek. Gladly. What stories are in these sighing moans? What thoughts never spoken or feelings expressed? We hold hands. I speak; tell her how much her quiet, steadfast, loving strength has meant to me all these years. Of course, I am crying, just as I am now. She turns her face towards me and there is Getty, looking at me, blue eyes clear and alive. "I love you, Ann."

"I love you too, Getty," and I lean forward to tuck my head into her shoulder.

I find myself in the hammock with a young Aunt Gertrude telling stories about her childhood with her sisters and brothers, and about Cheltenham.

ARRIVING

Spring
This is how my child's story of Cheltenham always begins. It's a Sunday in early spring of 1936, the roads almost bare of snow and warm enough for a road trip. That means a first of the season lunch at Cedar Close with "The Aunts" as we call them. I and my younger sister Jane — a plump, fair not quite six

to my dark-haired twiggy seven-year-old frame — pile in to the back seat of the Ford sedan. We set out from our suburban North Toronto home on the 36-mile drive northwest to the tiny village of Cheltenham to visit my mother Grace's unmarried sisters, Damaris and Gertrude (Getty) Beattie.

A long drive through gently rolling countryside — Jane and I count cows or join Dad and Mom as they sing old favourites like "Swing Low Sweet Chariot" and "Good Night Irene" or the latest hits like "Red Sails in the Sunset" and "Pennies From Heaven."[2] Then a right turn from the now boring Highway #9 in Caledon Township to tree-lined Creditview Road. Swooping down the hill our high voices call out the names of familiar places: Station Rd. (to the tiny "flag your stop" station on the hill); the Anglican and United churches on our right, one with gingerbread trim, the other plain, as suits their persuasions; the Cheltenham General Store on the left, stone-built in 1877, now the village's oldest building in the valley where the village itself lies.

Cheltenham, founded as a mill town in 1822 on the banks of the Credit River, is northwest of Brampton. Even in the pre-war years, as history will name that time, and not yet post-Depression, Cheltenham is a small place, a scattering of buildings easy to miss. A gas station, several houses on either side of the country road, a few more on John St., then an unpaved track wandering to the left, across the Credit River, and we are in the outskirts again. Up a steep hill now, car window open, I watch for the high, impenetrable cedar hedge, smelling it before I see it. Voices stilled a moment for the sharp right turn on a blind hill into the driveway just past the hedge. Dad hates that turn, especially when we back out, Damaris standing sentinel on the other side of the track.

And there they are, waiting for us on the front porch, the green wooden floor and steps and the white railings in their springtime coat of paint. Damaris: slim, salt and pepper hair, blazing blue eyes like her father's (but I would never have said so), quirky sideways smile, in a smart sweater and a skirt of her own tailoring — I remember shades of navy, blue, and mauve with a touch of red. Gertrude, five years younger, half a step behind: round face, pink cheeks, china blue eyes. She wears plain, simply cut dresses that

Damaris makes for her in flowered prints whose colours change with the seasons, though even then they were a touch traditional.

Damaris had bought Cedar Close for a song from a cheese-maker in 1934 as a weekend retreat from her busy teaching life in Hamilton. My father had his doubts: "Damaris, you will never get the smell of cheese out of this house." My aunt was very fond of my father. Nevertheless, to be told by anyone — man or woman — that she could not do something was sure to produce the opposite. Leaving home at seventeen, Damaris, now in her late thirties, had long since learned to navigate her determined way through domestic and professional worlds with pleasant courtesy.

She began renovations in the cellar, clearing out years of another life's debris. When I'm eight I am allowed to go down the no hand-railing wooden stairs to fetch pickles for lunch. I look around in amazement at the shelves that line the walls, light let in from the below-ground window bouncing off the summer's preserves and jams in gleaming rainbow rows. A nose-tickling smell from the geranium roots strung upside down from the wooden beams mingles with the bouquet of medicinal herb bundles hanging beside them. They look so merry with their code-coloured wool bindings. The vinegary taste of pickles in crocks wrinkles my tongue, along with the lingering sweetness of last year's dandelion wine-making. But there is no curdled cheese smell, no trace of the cheese-maker who had lived there for years, except for the hard-packed dirt floor. You can crack a dish on that floor as I learn the remorseful day when I misjudge my step in the one-light-bulb shadows:

"Are you all right dear?" from the lit doorway at the top of the steep stairs.

Hurried steps. A pat on the top of my head, "A quick mop up now, we'll just get another dish-full," as Damaris takes my hand, letting me carry the brimming dish in the other one.

"I've been meaning to put another light down there," she says ruefully to my mother. As if she's at fault, not me!

On our next visit I see that I will still be able to go down the cellar stairs. Damaris has found a way to keep us safe, rather than forbidding an adventure. As well as another light she has made a plain wood railing for the narrow stairs. It isn't as elaborate as the one rising from the first to second floor. She turned the spooled uprights for that one on a lathe in the workshop reserved for boys at the school where she taught domestic science to the girls and learned other useful skills on the boys' side of the school.

It was clear to me, even then, that when money is scarce, and there's no other way to get something done, you find a way to do it yourself. But I was too young to realize how unusual it was for her to occupy the male world of tools and machines.

A lunch of a casserole and the first asparagus — "Those spindly, tasteless spears you see in the supermarket are the last of the season, not the first," one of them is sure to sniff — with rhubarb crumble or upside-down cake for dessert. Then a tour of the glorious front gardens. Damaris's labour of love, a praise-song to beauty in the midst of daily frugalness and practicality, she has designed and built them from an untended meadow that had to be stumped and de-rocked. Damaris rode the tractor that pulled the stumper, an unbelieving Mr. Henry, her near neighbour, hovering close by. He loved the story, eager to tell anyone who would listen, "She near severed a foot the time she fell off, but she climbed right back on. She's a wonder, that one!"

In just three years the rocks pile up into a low dry-fence at the back of the garden. Shaking his head at the scope of Damaris's ambitions, Mr. Henry rumbles the turf away in his horse-drawn wagon to anyone who needs fill. The first beds take shape on either side of the renovated screen porch at the side of the house where the gangly hollyhocks grow now. What will be the showcase perennial beds curve, one scallop a season, as work-time and money permit, around the sunny half of the grassy space. A spring bulb and summer shade garden near the hammock under the trees stretches to the cedar hedge that gives the cottage its name, "Cedar Close." No flowerbeds here. Even lawn-planted herbs like ground-thyme can't grow in soil leached of nutrients and moisture from the greedy, water-sucking cedars.

During her teaching years Damaris lived near the Botanical Gardens in Hamilton and could buy the culls. "Not inferior plants," she says firmly, but "surplus to their needs."

Roses of every colour and size bloom in profusion throughout the season. There are heritage roses, including Grandma Beattie's pale pink single with the yellow centre that grows from a root brought from Scotland. Her family, descended from the Monnies, a branch of Clan Menzies, emigrated to Hamilton, Ontario, in 1874, when Margaret Rodger was only a year old.

The Beatties were Presbyterian Scotch-Irish originally from Kilrea, County Derry, Northern Ireland. I remember my grandfather's arrivals at our home in Toronto. James Campbell Beattie — J.C. I to the family — is on his own in 1937. A stern, unyielding Plymouth Brethren pastor who brooked no intransigence from parish or family, his unpredictable bursts of violent temper were legendary and feared. He was also an itinerant preacher, walking between towns in winter to preach to PB congregations.

Retired at 70, he is still "one tough man" as his son Campbell said years later, tall, upright, and vigorous, no cane, no hat on his full head of white hair, even in winter. Those blazing blue eyes. Every year I hope that he will bring me a different present for Christmas. Every year it's another Christian tract. "Written especially for children," he says with satisfaction at a gift well chosen.

My grandmother left her husband in 1935 to live with Gertrude in an apartment on Brunswick Ave. in Toronto as soon as she was sure the children were launched — a move that surprised no one but him. Watching him stride down the long, steep hill to our house I imagine conversations that might have been about when she would move:

"You won't go with him when he moves to Cleveland," one of them might say.

"I can't afford to stay here in this big house (in Barrie)."

"Getty and I will rent an apartment in Toronto. No, No! It will be fine."

Damaris reassures, *"You can help take care of the house and cook. I'll be in Hamilton most of the time anyway."*

Would she protest about being a burden?

"Getty will have more time to be at the hospital now that she

has greater responsibilities, and we won't be worrying about you any more. You'll see...."

There is a cutting from Grandma's rose in Gertrude's over-wintering balcony pots, in my mother's garden, in my gardens, in my sister's city and country gardens, as there will be later in her daughter Sophie's garden. Family garden-line, enduring woman-line, she climbs the southwest porch wall of the house mingling with deep purple and pink clematis — a rare cream and magenta "Nelly Moser" in pride of place.

We leave reluctantly with gifts of asparagus and rhubarb and perhaps a plant-root that is surplus to Damaris's garden needs, drive home with the afternoon sun behind us to our city lives — homework, dinner and an early bed to be ready for school and work — filled in every way with countryside abundance.

COUNTRY WEEKENDS: SUMMER

Friday Night, 1940

In the spring of 1940 our Cheltenham adventures with the aunts really begin. It's a year into the war and my father decides to sell the car; gas is rationed and too expensive when you can get it. Jane and I are allowed to travel, daringly by ourselves at ten and eleven — much admired by our peers — on the Friday afternoon train (yes, trains ran to many small villages then). We are solicitously handed down by the conductor on our arrival to the platform at the small country station where Damaris — and usually Gertrude — wait, backlit by the afternoon sun.

First stop is the General Store to buy the week's extras — groceries had been laid on earlier in Orangeville to take advantage of the mid-week sales — and for Gertrude and Damaris to catch up on the news. The proprietor always offers us "a little something" which, after a glance from the aunts, we save for later. No need to actually say, "You'll spoil your supper." Their heritage, and ours, is from a "deeds not words" deeply rooted Presbyterian background and that look tells us that "aunterly" indulgence goes only so far.

Into the car again and off up the hill to the house. The aunts take the bags in by the side door to start supper while Jane and I are happily left to our own devices. Depression and WWII-era parents seemed to say "careful" a lot, sheltering us from the back story until much later. We run around to the front, making a beeline for the striped cream and green cloth hammock strung between two trees snug by the hedge. We swing, sing, or bicker, or continue with another instalment of the adventures of the mythical Ann and Jane (whose parents were perfect and allowed all sorts of astounding adventures) that we had begun on the train to amuse ourselves on the journey.

Supper in the oven, town shoes changed to country brogues or rubber boots, Damaris and Gertrude snatch a quick tour of the flower beds and vegetable gardens to check for insect depredations and the week's growth. We watch from our swaying perch as, moving quickly and surely with secateurs in hand, heads bobbing among the tall stocks, they clip the fading blossoms from the dozen varieties of delphinium, singles and doubles in deep purple, mauve, rose, pink, yellow and white. The pride of the neighbourhood, and prizewinners at the annual Caledon Township Garden Show, they rise majestically in the middle of the perennial border soaring over the hybrid tea roses — and above the aunts. The broad, pointed leaves of irises are interplanted among the roses, fluted cups rising from plain and fringed beards in the more common purples, pinks, yellows and whites and then the rare ones in bronze and gold, or magenta stripes you could see nowhere else, except in the Hamilton gardens.

Friday's companionable supper is a "good" — we had lots of meat in wartime — usually beef or chicken stew cooked the night before and brought up in the cooler. New greens from the garden, the last of the year before's home-preserved fruit and then Getty's homemade cake or squares. If a smile can twinkle, hers does, as she offers seconds before we can ask. We decide the next day's chores together and discuss options for the Saturday excursion or social event: we are a part of their lives on the weekend and expected to be as involved and accommodating as they are.

When the days are long, we might pick the bright yellow heads for dandelion wine. Although Plymouth Brethren are teetotallers there was always dandelion wine "for visiting doctors and clergyman." "How come," I would wonder, "did a visiting Plymouth Brethren minister drink wine?" (Years later I learned from a cousin that J.C. I had been a secret brandy drinker.) It was the loveliest, translucent pale yellow, and said to be very potent. Damaris didn't easily part with favourite recipes but, grown up, I would ask her for this one. Somehow my wine never tastes like hers — something is missing. I would never have insulted her with a question about the difference.

One day, when my friend Barbara and I are visiting Damaris and sampling the dandelion wine, Barbara asks for the recipe. Damaris obliges. I listen carefully and hear an ingredient not in the recipe she'd given me. I cannot remember now what it was, but I do remember that Barbara's wine was almost as delicious as Damaris's and much tastier than mine! I told myself that it must have been that she forgot that ingredient when she gave me the recipe.

We walk the dog along the shoulder of the road before an early to bed for all of us. Up the green-painted, narrow wooden stairs to two bedrooms, one on each side of the landing, a linen closet at the head of the stairs, the bathroom at the back of the landing. I love the rose and mauve bathroom with matching coloured towels and old Ontario glass pieces for soap, nail brush and toothbrushes. Damaris's room is on the right, Gertrude's to the left, where we sleep. Gertrude's silver-backed brush and comb are on the dresser, her nightgown and dressing gown hang in the closet with a few dresses and a sweater. Clothes are not important to Getty: she had trained to be a missionary nurse; rheumatic fever ended that dream but not her choice of how she would live, or her first job with the China Inland Mission. She sleeps on a pull-out couch in the living room when we're there, although it's always made up before we are up. Both double beds are spooled, one an antique, one that Damaris has turned in the shop at school, covered in flower-patterned, hand-stitched quilts. On the bureaus, their embroidered runners and old silver dresser sets from the antique shop down the road, "picked up for a song, not many people want that kind of thing now." She loves a bargain.

Day's End

Teeth cleaned, hair brushed,
Jane and I
on the double bed
stretch legs
to meet sloped roof, toes
touch ceiling, noses breathe
"the Aunts' smell."
What is it?

Old wood and woodsmoke,
ironed linens, rose soap, herbs
and spices, sweetness
of yeast, sun on damp earth
in the morning — the essence
of aunts and Cedar Close.

We drift into sleep lulled
by sounds of the peaceful ordered
calm in the pattern
of Cheltenham days.

A last sigh and clank
of the sink-pump as Damaris
and Gertrude putter
in the kitchen, murmur
goodnight to the dog, the shhsh
of a car on the road, and the
thickness of unaccustomed dark.

Saturday Morning, 1944

Breakfast is porridge, oatmeal or Red River: unhealthy, expensive, packaged, sugared flakes are not considered. Bananas and raisins are sweetness enough. Then eggs, soft boiled or scrambled, toast and homemade jam — we can choose our favourite, even if it means opening a new jar.

Morning chores next. First the dishes. In Beattie households —

my mother's too — beds are made before you come downstairs, fully dressed, ready to greet a new day and whatever it holds in store. In a big family, you learn young to look after yourself, to help with the little ones, to ease your mother's workload. (Even now, for me, an unmade bed, or a day in pyjamas is the ultimate in self-indulgent sloth.) Then weed the garden. Straw hats in place to protect almost middle-aged complexions, Damaris and Gertrude look after the flowerbeds. At fourteen and fifteen, Jane and I have had enough lessons to take care of weeds in the big vegetable garden, a Depression and wartime necessity that becomes permanent in peacetime. It begins on the "back" side of the porch and runs right down the hill almost to the Credit River. The aunts can see our round-brimmed "camp hats" from Eaton's, where my dad was a buyer, from where they work.

By the time the hose is set in the day's place, the dog is prancing for a walk. She leaves the road's shoulder, pauses to refresh her mark and to sniff new smells while we chat with a neighbour "out front," usually Mrs. Henry, whose own ample front is always a source of wonder. While we're gone Damaris and Gertrude start that day's preserves in a huge kettle (as my mother does weekdays in her city kitchen). The heavy sweetness of simmering fruit and sugar drifts through the window that looks out over the porch to the garden.

My Family's Cellar Cold Room

A braced wooden door
across from the wash tubs.
I step down through shafts of drifting
dust motes lit from a window above ground
to packed earth and shelves of stacked colours.

Rows and rows of fruits put down in season,
multi-hued reds of rhubarb   strawberry   currants
raspberry   dark sweet cherries   amber pie cherries
pale yellow pears with cloved stems
orange peach halves   pink apple sauce
Tender vegetables wait at the back

preserved in big jars, feasts of carrots
beans   peas   asparagus   cauliflower.
Smaller jewelled jars of jams
Gooseberry to die for! Peach
with almonds and maraschino cherries.
Different jellies for toast, chicken and meat.

Mom's chili sauce
Grandma's famous plum chutney
passed down to a favoured few
queue in the front line with three cut
glass jars of Aunt D.'s Manhattan fruits
set apart for Thanksgiving, Christmas and Easter.

Four stone pickle crocks on the floor
Dad's special dills, Helen's sweet gherkins,
Uncle Phil's chunky mixed and
my favourite "bread and butter" slices.
Raised slats hold   Hubbard squash   turnips
potatoes sprouting eyes
some gone by February, others last
'til March. A long summer's sweaty work,
the precious jars go one by one.

Close the door,
keep in the cold   until
rose rhubarb nubs
and pale green asparagus spears
push through the last snow
in the back garden   time to plant
snow pea seeds under the trellis.

Lunch is set on the screened-in porch, where the quilting frame
rests in a corner. Step past the morning's garden tools to a cloth-
covered, green wicker table laden with homemade soup, fresh-
baked bread it must have been rising overnight. And real butter!
I remember asking Getty, "Where does the butter come from?"
Because butter was in even shorter supply than earlier in the war

and we ate margarine almost all the time.

With a little wink she replied, "Well, in the country there are ways to 'have some left over.'" I didn't quite understand what she meant but picked up from that wink that further investigation was out of the question.

We admire the morning-picked vegetables: I love the fat, red beefsteak tomatoes and corn from the patch that slopes down the hill to the river.

Saturday Afternoon Stories

An afternoon pause for a rest and reading. When we are little, on a day too hot to sleep upstairs, we might cuddle with one of the aunts, all three in the hammock, and tell stories: older, long-legged and gangly, one of us sits on the grass. We always want to hear about what life was like when they were young. They tell us about their mother's early school-teaching days when she was only eighteen, in a one-room schoolhouse, some students as old as she is. They tell us how lucky they and their siblings were, and now we are, in our schooling.

Monday laundry day was fascinating (to us). Some years there was a laundress-helper, most years it was the boys who filled the big copper kettle from the pump and heaved it on to the stove first thing in the morning so they — boys and girls — can hang out the clothes on long criss-crossing lines in the garden before they go to school. The children all had jobs to do; that was part of being in a family — boys as well as girls learned to cook and to mend.

They were frequently dirt poor when their father was on the road and Campbell often shovelled coal off the locomotive tender when it was going through town so they could have more coal for heating. Margaret Beattie had learned to be self-sufficient at an early age. Her marriage to an erratic, moody man who flew into terrible, unpredictable rages underscored her Scottish resolve to make sure her children were too. She knew they'd be on their own soon enough, probably with no more than a high school education, the boys maybe in the army, if looming European troubles came to war.

There were nine children born. Of the five boys, David died in

1911 when he was not quite two of diphtheria, a dreaded but common scourge at the time.

Jack came along three years later when Grace was twelve. She notes in her memoir,[3] "I took him over, trundled him around in his pram, told him stories, comforted him. He aroused and satisfied all my immature maternal instincts and I hated father when he was cross with him." Jack grew into a healthy, intelligent boy, "loveable, witty and terribly moved to pity," good at sports and with many other interests. Sadly, he sickened suddenly in 1928, the year Grace was married and expecting her first baby (me). He visited her in Toronto when he came down for doctors' appointments, admired her newlywed home, went downtown with Helen and bought a pair of bootees, asking: "Would these be suitable for the new baby?" They were a "precious gift" to Grace as is the Noah's Ark he carved for me, his newborn niece, painted blue and red. He died of leukemia later in 1929, "before he could make the animals." *I mourn the loss of my son to this day. To care for a new baby and to grieve and then mourn a beloved brother who was like a child to her would surely have taxed my mother's emotional resources to the limit.*

"The other sons left home as soon as they could to get away from their Plymouth Brethren minister father who resented his sons and did nothing to make them feel loved and wanted" — as Grace says in her Letters to Meggie.

Campbell, J.C. Beattie II, the oldest, born in 1899, was a mechanic in the Canadian Airforce. He moved to Cleveland, Ohio and became a mechanical engineer who observed complex surgical procedures and then made stainless steel operating instruments for them. He married "a quiet Christian woman" from a well-known Plymouth Brethren family in Cleveland and they had four children. When J.C.B. I announced a second visit, that "quiet Christian woman" made her own announcement: "I won't have that man in my house again. It's either him or me." Although J.C. I was never a welcome guest thereafter, and was heartily disliked by all of his children, his son Campbell looked after his father, especially in his single life, until he died. Campbell stayed with us when he came to Toronto twice a year from Cleveland to buy Dack's shoes for his oldest son, J.C. III. He was a tall, genial, caring man deeply connected to his brothers and sisters and spoke with what I thought of as an American accent. I loved his story-letters to us, the G's and Q's shaped like cats, their tails trailing down the pages.

Philip, born in 1912, alienated his father forever. They never spoke again. While following his father's ministerial profession he took a different path when he won a scholarship to Wycliffe College and took orders as an Anglican priest. Although "low church" Anglican, this was a form of Protestantism that his father considered almost Roman Catholicism, the dreaded "popery!": being told how to worship by a hierarchical group of elites that fundamentalist Christians like the Plymouth Brethren had rebelled against. Not to be tolerated. And certainly not in his family. Did he realize that disavowing his son was every bit as dictatorial as the Catholicism he loathed and feared because it deprived the individual of spiritual agency? Philip's fiancé was killed in the war and he never married. He was a fond uncle, visited us often, his laughter filling the room as he told stories of parish life and listened very seriously to our childhood and growing up triumphs and travails. I loved it that he relieved the stress of priestly life in twice yearly trips to New York to watch Marx Brothers and Charlie Chaplin movies. My mother went with him one time and said that his laughter boomed out across the entire theatre causing smiling patrons to look around for the source. I loved him very much and missed him terribly after he died, so young, at 48.

George was different from the others. Born in 1907, he was small and thin, with a darker skin, tense and wildly active. He would likely have been diagnosed as a hypertonic baby today. His father had no patience with him and sent him to Cleveland "just for the summer" when he was fifteen to work in his Uncle George's jewellery store. His father arranged for that job and home to be permanent and George never came home again. With a wonderful mind, but lacking an education, he had a series of jobs: banker, pilot, entrepreneur, making and losing money many times (when he was supported by his siblings) and finally a brilliant journalist. He worked hard and drank heavily with well-known journalists like Frank Tumpane and

J.V. McAree, married and had a son. I sat on his knee when he visited us, spellbound with stories of his life, but he ended his own at 41. That's when my mother told me why he had stopped coming to dinner. He broke a chair in our living room one night when he was drunk and my father banished him from the house. My father never knew that mother met her unhappy young brother for lunch every month, until he died. His wife Francis, a gifted teacher, and young son Paul, left for the States; they seemed to disappear, almost as if they had died too. Years later I read at a Heritage Site created by Campbell's son Jim Beattie that Paul had become a Unitarian minister. Still in the ministerial fold but the polar opposite to both "the Roman way" and fundamentalism.

The family was poor, the children, isolated from their peers, made their own fun. Swimming in Kempenfelt Bay near Barrie in the summer, hikes and picnics in the countryside. In winter the boys made skates and fast iceboats from cast-off sleds, skate runners and sails from old sheets and took the girls sailing on the bay. They knew not to say how scared they were or they would not have been asked again.

Damaris was the oldest girl; born in 1900 she too left home as soon as she could. I was entranced whenever she talked (not often) about her training in "the rag trade" in New York. As a child I could not know the tough, hard life she would have had as a young single girl learning "a trade" in a poorly paid, highly competitive industry. But I was awestruck at her courage to risk being alone at only seventeen in 1917 in the big city. Little knowing her straightened circumstances then, I imagined her living a glamorous life in New York, envied her knowing how to make wonderful clothes cheaply (my sister will do that in Paris). I don't know what drew her back but she was successful enough to land a job teaching sewing and cooking at Hamilton Central Tech, in her mother's first home town as it turned out.

My clever, witty mother Grace, born in 1902, was the second of the four daughters and the only one who married. She was the first child in the family to go to university, read English and history in 1926 thanks to Miss Keagy, a teacher who supported her financially. She became a copywriter to discharge her debts and then qualified as a teacher, like her mother and grandmother. She kept a home for us and for visiting brothers and sisters, entertained our friends. "Did the boyfriends come to see us or for her famous butter tarts and lively conversation?" I would wonder, and admire. She proofread our essays, wrote stories we didn't know about, read deeply, loved unsparingly, never proselytized her Anglican faith and rarely mentioned her failing heart. Nor did she talk about her abiding sadness in the loss of three brothers until her poignant cry much later in Letters to Meggie:[4] "I would give my few remaining years to have an hour's conversation with George, or Jack or Philip. Those three were the dearest in my whole life. My children I [love] deeply, devotedly but they of course — and quite rightly — regard me with a more critical eye."

Gertrude — born in 1905 — was a tranquil person with a quick, dry sense of humour. She steadied Damaris's more mercurial and sometimes irascible temperament. She was a whiz with numbers — would have been a chartered accountant today. When early heart problems meant that nursing was no longer an option for her she worked as secretary-treasurer in a series of progressively more responsible (but not much more remunerative) positions. When I was thirteen in my first summer job at the old Sick Children's Hospital, horrified at the cockroaches scurrying out from under the radiators in the "tap" room, she told me her own hospital stories. Getty had loved nursing, spoke longingly of the rewards, but with my first glimpse of a beaten child I know I will never have the kind of courage Gertrude has, could never train to be a missionary nurse. But, "*What kind of missionary? What countries would you have lived in?*" I wonder. Later, her travel journals and letters to my mother revealed her "itchy foot," her joy in visiting other countries and observing other cultures.

The girls snuck forbidden "un-Christian" books into their room to read in secret, wary of their father who prayed with one eye open during morning and evening prayers to make sure theirs were obediently closed. All of them walked quietly to church on Wednesday nights and twice on Sunday. Grandfather was the pastor of the only Plymouth Brethren church in Barrie, a stricter than Calvinist sect: no dancing, no singing, no card playing, no candles scenting the air, no reminding cross. J.C.'s stipend is left in the collection plate after the sermon except when he was travelling to preach — *what did they live on then?* It better be a good sermon, and the family must be "good" too. They were "pastor's kids," their mother the "pastor's wife," setting a Christian example in the small community — and teased and shunned in their neighbourhood, and at school. "*When did they laugh and play?*" I'd wonder. *Ice-boating? Reading forbidden books? There must have been other times to make them into the laughing women I heard in the kitchen when they came to dinner. Just in the kitchen?*

Helen, the baby, was born in 1917. She was like her older sisters' child (they were seventeen, fifteen and twelve) and a big sister for me, born twelve years later. We played duets together and in my teens would sneak upstairs for a forbidden cigarette. She trained as an occupational therapist, joined the army with the WRNS and was posted overseas. There are smiling pictures of her in uniform on leave in London, and after the war she helped set up the Occupational Therapy Department for war veterans at Sunnybrook Hospital. These must have been traumatic experiences but I don't remember ever hearing her talk about them. Later she worked in a Montreal hospital as an occupational therapist. She became more distant for me, seemed to be the most independent of them all in the sense of living "away" all of her adult life. Growing up in boring Toronto — quiet and staid, a very different city than it is now — I'd love to have heard more about life in Montreal. But she kept a very private life and her visits to Cheltenham are usually troubled with bronchitis or pneumonia and are few and far between.

There are fewer stories when we're no longer children. Jane and I read on the porch, on a blanket on the grass or in our bedroom under the eaves, a leafy summer-green or autumn-gold nest, to dream our own adventures. We might hear bits and pieces about their daily life in city and country in casual conversation, but talk about their personal lives, growing up and as adults, is not their habit. I know them, and my mother and their brothers, through the recreated images of their stories that I take with me to savour until the next visit, from my observing senses and by a sort of familial osmosis, the way children do, of the way they lived their lives. *The epitome of "deeds not words."*

When I am curious about their "not at Cheltenham lives," which is most of their lives, all they say is that Damaris teaches sewing and cooking at Hamilton Central Technical School, and Gertrude is a secretary-treasurer at the China Inland Mission. One time I overheard Damaris talking with mother about a threat to her job. The Hamilton Board had decided that all teachers must have a teaching certificate, which Damaris does not have. She tells mother that her principal threatened to leave if she had to, and "that was the end of that," she says, with considerable relief. I know that Gertrude "loves to go to bed with a set of books to get them right" just as Philip does, but just how they "keep track of where the missionaries are" at the China Inland Mission is a mystery to me. Gertrude is not forthcoming with any more details.

I know them through silence. Their silence is like a calm, untroubled lake of everyday living with only the occasional dark, shoreline bubble disturbing the surface. Like the reference to their father as "a very bad-tempered man," the only reference to him that I recall them making. Stories of his brutality and rejection surface much later in the letters and memoirs of other family members.[5] As well as the stories we heard about their childhood they tell me how my grandmother was the first to teach sign language in Barrie, and was known for other "good works." But her enduring support of her children, and their deep love for her that I sense through their stories, is not spoken, or expressed physically. It comes through in the way that I know they love us, in how we care for one another, like welcoming Jane and me on weekends, which will also give my mother a break, and making us feel an important part of their lives. Like making sure their mother has a comfortable old age — and knowing what that is for her. There is no talk about what it was like to be a child in a "Christian" family of nine "keeping up appearances ... so important to father" while living near the poverty line, or for my grandmother to bear and raise nine children, and lose two (mercifully, she died before George did), or to live with a bad-tempered man. Or decide to leave him.

I can only imagine now, from the depths of my own losses and disappointments, what she must have felt.[6] My mother did tell me one day that she had married "to raise normal children" from the background she grew up in. She must have hoped that we would have no part of the legacy she carried with her. Why the other sisters did not take that risk is pure speculation. It could have been the scarcity of men after the killing fields of WWI. Perhaps it was the distrust of men laid down by their father — notwithstanding the brothers they adored. After all, they were women in a male-dominated, authoritarian era and may not have wanted the costs of living a life like their mother's. Perhaps they were "inclined to the single life" as lesbians were referred to in their day. One day when Getty and I were talking about the history of heart disease that killed the women in their family I asked her, "Then why do you think you and Damaris have lived so much longer than Grace?" who died at 67.

"I think it's because we never had children," she replied, neatly summarizing the stressful and often dangerous lives pre birth control that women led.

"Are you ever lonely?" I dared to ask Damaris one time about her single life.

"Of course" she says, "who isn't, from time to time?"

As a gangly, uncoordinated kid with glasses and a love of books that separated me from most of my classmates until I was at university, and, at the time of our conversation having lived many years as a single woman, I know what she means without either of us saying another word.

After the mid-day break it's time for a Saturday afternoon excursion. We might walk to a neighbour's, perhaps the Henry's, or to the antique shop. Aunt D. could have spotted a piece of Georgian silver, fine bone china or pink lustre earlier in the week that was being kept until Saturday. The bargaining was so polite I didn't realize what was going on until I was in similar situations later in my life, having caught the collecting bug, and found myself haggling like a pro to get what I wanted in a friendly way.

There is a memorable trip to The Badlands, near Ingersoll. Now under the care of The Bruce Trail Association.

"Why bad?" I ask. "The rolling red hills and gullies are beautiful."

"Yes they are" said one of the aunts, "but you can see. Nothing can grow here."

The countryside around us is rich and fertile, as I do see on another trip to the lovely village of Belfountain to look at the little cottage on the banks of the meandering Credit River Grandmother and Gertrude rented before there was Cedar Close. We visit a friend's pottery: everyday pots, mugs and plates for sale with the more expensive sculptures tucked amongst shrubs or at the foot of trees. City girl, learning that the land feeds body and soul.

We often drive to Grace and Don Elliot's cattle farm in nearby Chinguacousy Township. My parents, both with rural roots, had earlier taken my sister and me on a weekend "farm vacation" to have a sense of what farm life is like. "Helping" in barn and fields was arranged but it was pretty contrived and not quite what my parents expected when our hostess asked us to "save yerse forks, there's pie" at lunch. The Elliots are the only working farmers we got to know well enough to be aware of the satisfactions and hardships of that unpredictable life. We admire Mr. E.'s dreamy, big-eyed cows, look around the barn and realize how much work it is as he tells us what it takes to keep them healthy. We stroke the horses, their equestrian daughter's pride and joy, and dream of galloping over the hills. After a look at the latest prize ribbons we sit around the oval table in the parlour to a bountiful tea of sandwiches, scones with butter and jam, and a cake with lots of icing. Grace E. is not only a quintessential farmer's wife, she is community activist, church fundraiser, bridge partner, afternoon sherry companion, and Damaris's close friend whose support will be crucial to her independence as she ages.

On really hot days we putter around the property, or go down to the river, a sun-clear golden brown from years of falling leaves, to make leaf boats. We might chat with a local fisherman or wave to the occasional paddler. Damaris did not own a boat so we didn't paddle that river, nor did we swim, even on hot days; "You never know what's in the water," they'd frown. I didn't think of questioning them because I knew there would have been no money for boats and no place to rent one. We are never told to be careful but once in a while a voice floats over the garden or down the hill, "Ann? Jane?" Echoed with, "Over here. At the river."

On rainy days afternoon tea is at home, often with the next-door neighbours, the Baptist Church minister, his wife and children. From childhood we are included in these more formal occasions, as we are for whatever else happens on weekends. Guests come directly into the living room through the door from the front porch. The needlepoint fireplace screen is set to one side. Damaris gave it to me as a housewarming gift when we moved to our second home in 1958, and then reclaimed it, saying she "has a use for it" and will leave it to me in her will. Mercurial for sure. Surely not intransigent? I shrugged, avoiding what that might be telling me about her.

Afternoon Tea

Brass-handled fireplace tongs
shovel and whisk, glimmer in the flames.
Plump petals on the Moss Rose porcelain,
sunlit — afternoon fires are for company.

Pink and bronze lustre china
old-etched glassware line
walnut-wood shelves, rest
casually on inlaid side tables —
children don't seem to break things
in Damaris's home. We sit
around the oval tea table in sofa chairs
upholstered in flowered, period fabrics.

Tea is fine Indian, mostly milk for us,
scones with fresh butter and Cedar Close jam,
triangles of sugar-crunchy cinnamon toast,
homemade cookies and "The Cake"
a marvelous confection of vanilla pudding
in a batter that somehow stays light

fluffy, layered and topped
with meringue. Slices carefully placed
on china plates, tasted,
one mouth-watering bite at a time,
from silver dessert forks.

No matter how old we are, long past the "doll stage," we always ask Aunt Getty to make us a string of paper cut-outs. Even when her daily memory begins to fade the scissors flash in the firelight, sailors or dancers, bears or birds emerge expertly and magically in a lovely, long, white, dancing stream, memories to loop around the bed-post at home.

Toronto afternoon teas, with Grandmother and Getty in the living room of their apartment on Brunswick Avenue (costs shared with Damaris) is a pocket handkerchief of country in the city. They garden in pots on the balcony, fertilize the flowers with a bird's fallen feather. There is a hammock for us, strung between a porch-post and a huge, overhanging tree, voices rise and fall, spoons clink on china, teapot lids settle, radiating, at least for me, calm, peace, order and beauty. My child's memory of them is of gentle, tranquil women and the cool-warmth of Grandmother's hands as mine linger in hers.

"Never file your nails," she murmurs, "cut them with good nail scissors so they will be fine and strong."

I like to imagine that she enjoys holding hands as much as I do.

But she must have been a tough, assertive woman to simply up and leave a husband — unheard of for a woman in those days, let alone a good Plymouth Brethren. She was firm in her opinions, even letting a daughter-in-law know that she didn't think she was bringing up her children properly. I was told much later by one of those children that his mother had "packed up and left, hurt and angry and didn't visit Grandma in Barrie again." My cousin and I speculated: was it too much or not enough religion? Or about education, which she was passionate about? It could have been all of those, we agreed.

And Gertrude? The third of four sisters, she had worked out her own peaceable way to live co-operatively, keeping her own counsel unless asked, stepping back when necessary. She did not like open conflict. She quietly went her own way while resolute in her convictions and in her devotion to family and profession.

Evening

There is usually roast chicken with all the trimmings on Saturday night, cold for Sunday lunch unless there are guests. By the time I am a young teenager I look forward to dinners with the aunts' friends; the food is wonderful and we are drawn into the conversation with attentive questions about what they know of our lives gleaned from the aunts. It seems they "boast us" a little? When the tone of the conversation changes imperceptibly we know to make a graceful exit and retreat to the second floor and a book. As soon as they're settled with coffee and after dinner drinks, we creep down to the place on the landing that can't be seen from downstairs to listen. Not so much because of what they're talking about — politics, education, and health care don't interest us much then — but the way they talk.

I grew up in a time when women deferred to men, especially in public. While tempers might flare, Mom never makes a disparaging remark to or about my dad, even when he snaps "Where does the money go?" when he's figuring out how much of each monthly bill they can afford to pay. He'll roar a bit when he reads the *Evening Telegram* at night. Jane and I sit on the chesterfield across from his chair and wait for the paper to shake and for some choice bit of condemnation about current political chicanery. I often overhear mother and a friend (also a university grad) discuss articles they read in the *London Times* or the *New York Times* or laugh over the wonderfully eccentric letters. They are animated and often passionately engaged, but we rarely hear an angry argument or even a "heated" discussion.

At least not the kind we hear from our perch on the stairs. The aunts and their friends argue with each other. Sometimes get quite testy. Even unapologetically loud. Social security issues were hotly discussed — all of them had experienced poverty and insecurity as a result of the Depression and World War Two. Marion Hilliard was a prominent, ahead-of-her-time gynecologist at Women's College Hospital, and author of *A Woman Doctor Looks at Love and Life; Women and*

Fatigue. She had seen the effects of poverty and social class issues for women and children. She was the only one of the group who could persuade Charlotte Whitton, the first female mayor of Ottawa and life-long crusader for social welfare — and a hockey player — to climb off her political soapbox without making her feel that she shouldn't be passionate about her convictions. Charlotte, a dedicated Conservative, crossed party lines in her adamant support of the new Employment Insurance introduced in 1940, and never received another party appointment. Tall, quiet Eva Coon, Director of the YWCA, no stranger to women's insecurity and misery, can silence everyone with a well-considered point. I can hear the rise and fall of their voices now as I remember my first bird's-eye view of a different way a woman can be:

"But you cannot expect people who don't know what it's like to barely scrape by..."

"You certainly can, anyone with a shred of sense..."

"Or a modicum of compassion..."

"Well, it's going to take a lot of persuasion ..."

"And which party do you suppose has the political will..."

"That's pretty obvious, the CCF (Cooperative Commonwealth Federation, later the NDP) of course..."

"Oh come now, whoever is going to buy into that — it's too long a shot..."

"Doesn't matter, they are our political conscience..."

The details of the subject matter were beyond me at the time but conversations like this showed me that you can cook, clean, sew, quilt, garden, entertain and do all of these well, and also have a mind that shines at more than bridge, church meetings or the new book clubs. Even more of an eye-opener is that you can be unmarried and contentedly happy. They all live modestly — their salaries always less than men in similar positions — but save money to travel every few years. In the aunts' circle of friends — village and city — no one remarks if her lifelong companion is a woman as Dr. Hilliard's is. They talk lovingly about their families, are at one time or another the unmarried daughter who cares for ill or aging ones. But even as a youngster it doesn't escape my notice that being unmarried also carries unusual freedoms for a woman: a career, independence, time to follow one's interests, the benefits of disposable income, unfettered friendships.

When did my mother Grace write the stories I found in a brown leather portfolio after she died of a heart attack at 67 in 1970? Only then do I realize that she too was a pioneer. In her own way she followed her passion, underground and unheralded.

Sunday, 1946

There are fewer visits to Cheltenham over the next many years but Cheltenham and the aunts continued to be a haven. I remember when I was seventeen and heartsick, in the totally taken-over way that only a teenager can be, driving to Cheltenham with Getty on a Saturday night in June. My father has tried to explain why my sister's summer dreams of apprenticing on an archeological dig will be financed, but not mine to study French with a family in Quebec. I *understand* that there is not enough money for both, nevertheless I *feel* second best and discounted. A weekend with the aunts seems a sorry compensation and we drive in silence for miles. I know Getty is aware of the issue — in the way my family somehow circulates the unspoken — and it's obvious that I'm unhappy, but she offers no rationalizations for parental actions, asks no questions, doesn't try to help make me feel better. In the comfort of our silence, of not having to explain or talk about my feelings, I realize that this quietness carries no implication that I should be accepting and understanding and cheerful when I am not any of these. An ego-centered teenager becomes aware that all silences are not imposed, of the difference between silence and quiet, and that there are times when openness is not welcome. Or needed. Even though it does make telling a story difficult, I say now to Getty's shade. Arriving in time for lunch I sink into the easy, comfortable routine of Cheltenham.

Damaris and I tour the garden I haven't seen in a month or more. White daisies and black-eyed Susan are up now, as the delphiniums begin to fade, with rosemary shrubs doing well — Gertrude's prizes gathered on her travels to the misty English coasts of Devon and Cornwall — mine will never be more than a respectable plant size. Sweet William scents the fringed borders with other biennials planted to fill the gaps, and several purple coneflowers that always drive the bees crazy. I remember hearing their hummy buzz in blended harmony with Damaris's and Gertrude's voices all the way over to the hammock. Four or five varieties of oregano, sage and savoury are thriving — picked daily for salads and stews. Lavender and tiny white-star sweet cicely flowers in their emerald green nests crowd lady's mantle — a tincture made from the flower protects the skin from sun damage — the round, peach-fuzz leaves hold shining beads of morning dew for at least an hour. The tender basils, green and hard-to-grow purple, snipped to sprinkle on ripening tomatoes with a pinch of sugar, sit in pots tiered down the side porch steps near the kitchen so they can be brought in quickly at the first sign of a heavy rain or frost.

We three women get dinner, enjoy good food and digestible dinner-time talk. Getty tells me about her job at the Queen Elizabeth Hospital for Incurables. We agree that it's a detestable name. The hospital was established in 1874 to lessen the burden that long-term care patients, or those with untreatable diseases, formerly incarcerated in the local House of Industry, imposed on the city's main hospital, the Toronto General. It was a more humane solution, but the underlying message was clear, that the dying and chronically ill were still to be segregated from the rest of the population. When I visit Getty in her new apartment, she tells me that the hospital provides the residence as part of her position. I realize for the first time that she had set aside an independent life of her own to help give her mother ten years of untroubled contentment until she died. Neither of them cast worried looks my way. I am relieved, knowing that nothing will be said. Dishes, walk the dog, to bed with a book. I can't put my feet on the ceiling any more, but I am enveloped in woodsmoke, chicken stock simmering, voices murmuring. And sleep.

I wake to Sunday morning noises of coffee beans being ground, bacon sizzling and the sound of voices that seem never to have gone to bed. An early riser myself I stay in bed for awhile to leave them to a little early morning peacefulness, perhaps needed to prepare for the working week ahead, or to ease the effects of the heart problems that crippled them both in later life.

We skip church — it will take most of the morning and we'll be leaving after lunch as usual. But church is an important part of the aunts' lives in Cheltenham. They are members of the Anglican congregation up the hill past the General Store, not the Baptist church across the road from Cedar Close more closely aligned to the practices of their childhood. Although away during the week, they are fully involved in church activities: finance and fundraising for Gertrude, Damaris's quilting circle, bake sales, luncheons and the annual bazaar — all respected and welcomed ways to be part of the village community. Every year Gertrude crochets tea cozies for Cheltenham and Toronto bazaars from a pattern her mother gave her and she gives me. Twenty-five proper, tight-fitting cozies with places for handle and spout. Damaris makes all her clothes and most of Getty's: beautifully cut and lined coats, skirts, and trousers for her. People line up to buy her afghans and smocked dresses at the bazaar. Tea cozies and hand-sewn clothes will elicit oohs and ahhs, and murmurs of "The Miss Beatties always bring such lovely work."

After admiring the summer's work-in-progress Gertrude and I pick vegetables to take home; Damaris has made cold chicken with the first zucchini relish and salad for lunch. We munch the last of the homemade bread, the crusty ends so good with jam.

"It doesn't keep well after a few days," Damaris laughs.

"Eat up the last of the squares too."

"No point in packing a few," Gertrude and I chorus her familiar words.

YOU CAN BE BOTH AND SEE ONLY ONE, 1948–1960[7]

"There are times you just have to get through," as Damaris would say, and I did, through five lonely, out-of-place years of high school. Then four grateful, wonder-filled years of university, of not being afraid to have a brain and "coming into my own." Marriage soon after graduation to a man who listened, wrote poetry and good stories and gambled and drank. I thought that was all part of male university life, and temporary. Four children born from 1952–1959. A root from the Nelly Moser clematis is the first plant in the garden of our first house in Don

Mills in 1955, Damaris's voice in my ear with the details of the special care that distinguishes it from the other clematis varieties growing by its side. "Never cut a Nelly Moser before spring."

We spend summer holidays and most weekends at my husband's family island in the Kawarthas, enjoying close visits there with my parents as well. Mother bakes bread in the old woodstove we kept in the kitchen after we bought an electric range, gauging the temperature by when the hairs on her arm "tingled" when she put it in the oven. My father loved to pour us a "holiday beer" when the "sun was over the yardarm." He had learned to love retirement after he founded a small, volunteer company where he could happily use his consulting skills. These are the happiest of family times in a marriage that was beginning to crack open on the fault lines of addiction.

Although absorbed in city and cottage family life, it seems natural to mark family highlights at Cheltenham with Damaris and Gertrude: engagement and new baby pictures are taken there, the aunts smile in the background, provide tea and cakes, embroidered linens, wedding quilts like the one on my bed, knitted baby clothes, a silver spoon and cup, smocked dresses, a different colour for each girl-child. My children play in the gardens, learn to like dirt and worms and the skills of making do. They sway in the hammock telling stories, creak back and forth in the old-fashioned, green-painted wooden swing: slatted seats, with backs on either side, long enough for a child to lie down on, wide enough for the first engagement photograph ... Not quite the same. Always the same....

Until October 1960 and the phone call from Aunt Helen in Kelowna.

Years before, in a visit to Montreal, I had met the man Helen thought she would marry; learned on a later visit that she had refused him because he was a communist at the beginning of the McCarthy era, and they were too different to allow for a life together. When heart problems prevented her from full-time professional work, she became her brother Philip's hostess and chatelaine, first in his appointment as Canon of the Anglican Cathedral in Victoria, B.C., and then as Bishop of Kelowna, a mission diocese whose financial affairs needed to be put in order before it could become autonomous. Just the job for Philip who, like Gertrude, loved to tackle a set of financial books and move the columns from red to black. It was called a "donkey diocese" because of the constant travel and the steady diet of ham and scalloped potatoes provided by the good women of each parish — which Philip said prophetically "will do me in one day."

We know that Philip has serious digestive problems. We have not heard that he is dying of intestinal cancer, at only age 48, until Helen calls on October 4 to say that Grace should come. Damaris and Gertrude know, are already there, have arrived to gather around him together for their last visit and goodbyes. Without Grace. Philip has asked, "Where is Grace?" Mother tells me later, and when he does, Helen phones her. *Why only then?* Knowing he was so ill, why did they wait so long? My mother calls me in great distress; she and Philip have been devoted to each other all their lives, especially since the deaths of Jack and George, and she is desperate to see him. I am too: Philip has been a loving mentor to me for as long as I can remember and knows me in ways that parents cannot. *His gentle inquiry, when I was driving him to the airport, about whether I should marry C. He must have seen his beloved but alcoholic brother George in my young fiancé when love blinded me to the obvious.* But I am mother of four, one still an infant, and anyway, there is money for only one airfare. It is October 6th by the time everything is arranged, the plane makes a Vancouver stop before Kelowna and when Grace arrives Philip is unconscious. She sits beside him until he dies on October 8th. She thinks he squeezes her hand. Hopes desperately that he knew she was there. Is destroyed at the thought that he might not have.

My shock at how these beloved women in my life could hurt their own sister so grievously, my mother's pain at their betrayal, and her anguish that Philip might have died thinking she did not care enough to be with him, and my recognition of how deeply she suffered — that she could suffer so much comes out of nowhere. A dark family underside whose occasional glimpses I had consigned to the past, and have never imagined possible as part of the women I so love and admire, engulfs me. I have known them and the world they shared with me, in the direct, sensuous way a child sees the world. Growing up, they have been exemplars of an expanded womanhood that I didn't grasp about my mother in our more conventional-seeming home. Since they so rarely talk about themselves I have no inkling about their relationships with each other or of my mother's iconoclastic side. Naïvely I assumed that the aunts and my mother were as loving and kind with each other as they were with me. I was brought up — by parents and aunts — not to ask questions about family matters. But, of course, I had asked *myself* quite a few over the years and had come to realize in my thirties that values around hard work, frugality, practicality, independence, family loyalty, while not "dwelling on unpleasantness" were fundamental to aunts and parents alike. They were just practiced differently in the lives they had chosen.

But the aunts not allowing my mother to say goodbye to a brother she had loved deeply has no place in the narrative I have lived with them and I am heartsick. I close myself to the intrusive and troubling desire to understand why they did what they did. Even now, in writing this, I am seized with a heaviness in my chest that is almost disabling. So "strong a disinclination," as my grandmother would say, that it is several days before I can continue to write. Picking up the thread of the story again, I struggle with the "unspeakable," the unspoken injunction to never expose family business, air dirty laundry, discuss personal life or reveal personal inadequacies.

I do not ask myself how their grief for a brother beloved by them, as well as by Grace, can so blind them to their own actions. Helen is losing a brother who made a home for her that provided a comfortable personal and social life when she could no longer support herself. Damaris and Gertrude will grieve not only their loss, but their sister/child Helen's as well. They may well have perceived my mother as having many more to love. Or of intruding on their needs, taking away some of what little time there was for them to be with him. Were they jealous of Grace's relationship with Philip, of his wanting her to be there when he died? Even worse, what happened around his death — a man so loved by everyone — seems an awful thing to do to *him*, to allow him and his death to be associated with cruelty and betrayal.

At the time, I could make no sense of their behaviour; their closed-in silence bordered on the sadistic to me, a mockery of what they had taught me about family loyalty, closeness and caring: like Uncle Campbell looking after his dad even though it was well known that he didn't like or respect him. Like the aunts making personal and financial sacrifices to care for their mother. My anger and sadness about how Helen has hurt and betrayed my mother and indeed all of us spills into an outraged letter. She writes back to say she is sorry I feel that way. No explanation. Maybe she doesn't have one. Maybe she thinks it's none of my business. Maybe, as Arnold says dryly in Robert Hugh's *Hope Springs*,[8] "There are things in this life that you don't say for a reason." But I was not in the world of reasons.

We don't see much of each other for many years. The rest of us carry on almost as if nothing has happened, not bringing up an uncomfortable subject. I had not understood their behaviour, could not fathom the kinds of feelings that had aroused it, nor could I find a place in our lives together for my own feelings. My impulsive, rule-breaking outspokenness in the letter to Helen does not extend to questioning Damaris and Gertrude — obviously, from their point of view, I have done quite enough. In a way, I agreed. I had seen in them, and much worse, felt, the awful consequences of how "we can be both and see only one." I too did not want to "dwell on it." I wanted no tarnish to colour the treasured storehouse of images, impressions and questions that I draw on all the time during the next fifteen years. I carry with me the sounds of women talking, arguing and laughing, the everydayness of their resilience, perseverance, adaptability and strength. And beauty. And ambivalence.

Yes, I continue to be ambivalent about Damaris and Gertrude. I still want my children to know the nurturing comfort they have given me, to experience country and village life and to have a more direct sensuous experience of the natural world and of community that neither city nor cottage life give me, and I know will not provide for them. I tell my children: how Aunt Jane and I spent hours in the hammock telling our own stories, invented entire families of people and animals who spoke other languages and had adventures — brave, scary, romantic — just like the aunts told me they had when they were little and my mother too, with her family of imaginary friends that she told my daughter Meg about in a letter, how I would dream away an hour gazing at the populated sky: clouds, birds, insects in season, shivering colour-changing leaves and branches.

In 1967 my father is suddenly stricken with an aneurism. Sitting by his bedside I hold his hand. "Dad, do you know I'm here? Can you squeeze my hand back?" He does. We take turns, Mom, Jane and I, until he dies. I am bereft of the more physical parent who was unabashedly gleeful about his love for dancing and singing — so atypical of his Baptist upbringing. I feel hollowed out inside, yearn for one more companionable after-dinner walk when he and my mother come to visit. Far worse for my mother, his pension from the "benevolent" T. Eaton Co. dies with him and mother is in straightened circumstances. A clan gathers. The aunts are there: they visit, go out together, call frequently. I don't know how they do it without treading on my mother's fierce independence, but they manage to make her life a little more "comfortable." I "top it up" with casual groceries, rye whiskey for the Friday night bridge game and dinner out together whenever I can manage. My younger children are there every Friday to do the shopping and cleaning and afterwards to have tea and play Parcheesi, just as they had with their grandfather, keeping all of their memories of him alive. *I never speak of marriage problems and the probability of a divorce. I know that she is heartsick at her core and am loath to add anything more. Now I wonder at the family pattern of dealing with distress.*

Those children hardly know what to do with themselves on Friday nights, after my mother, their beloved grandmother, dies in September 1970, only 67. And I? It's windy around me, I am cold with feelings of abandonment, an orphan. Helen risks plane travel with her shaky heart. The aunts' faces, sagging in shock and pain, are rearranged to help us present a calm public face — seemingly effortlessly — and clearly show the two faces we all live. This time, far from duplicitous. It's how we manage. *It takes strength to hold this. And history.*

How did they know? What had they tackled to learn the professional skills and personal discipline to support and empower them all their lives? How generous they were to give us some of their "time-out" time so that our lives would be enriched by what country and village life offered. Stark contrast to their strange refutation of my mother's feelings, and the withdrawal of their own when Philip died: They are both, and at the time I saw only one. We are all both. They built a village community that accepted never-married single women — and what a contrast that was to their isolated, fundamentalist small-town community. How naïve and arrogant: wounded and heart-sore at a pantheon crumbling I had been, for one grievously hurtful act that I knew of, to hold them to a standard I knew by now that I could never attain, nor could anyone. They were ever alert to their great nieces and nephews, and to me, no matter what was happening in all of our lives.

Like my grandmother before me I had finally left an abusive, unhappy marriage. But I never felt that we were a "broken" family: remember now, with tears in my eyes, singing carols together on our first single-parent Christmas eve, just as we had always done.

"Where else would you go but to Cheltenham?" a friend asks, when I need a refuge during years of professional and personal stress, and to heal after an accident whose repercussions still inhabit me. Where else indeed when I feel like the earth under the cedar hedge at Cedar Close, sucked dry of nurturing and moisture, and fear to be a caring-burden to my adult children, as they prepared to leave home.

Autumn, 1974

By now Damaris is retired, but not Gertrude at 69. A few years before she retired from the Queen Elizabeth Hospital at 65 the director suggested she take a raise to improve her financial situation. She refused, saying that the hospital couldn't afford it. Her first post-retirement position was treasurer for the Anglican Church Home administered by the Sisters of St. John the Divine (SSJD), an order where my mother and Gertrude were lay associates. After a long-dreamt-of winter in the Canary Islands with friends, she is now in her second post-retirement career at the YWCA. Cheltenham is blessedly familiar whiffs of manure and woodsmoke, leaves swirling in shades from carrot to brick to crimson, carpets of new pine needles sharp green on last year's rusty floor. Outdoors we harvest vegetables and put the garden to bed in stages. By the first serious frost only parsnips, first-year leeks and hardy turnip will dot the naked beds.

We divide plants for redistribution in garden bare spots, in potted plants for indoor windowsills, or as gifts for my garden wrapped in damp newspaper and Damaris's instructions on how to plant them. "Nothing to it," she says, whacking through an iris or daisy root with a razor-sharp spade. That done, we clean garden tools, scour pots for bugs and mould and put them away on shelves in the "mysterious" Tool Shed, a small house at the back of the garden where Jane and I had played for hours populating it with our other family's adventures.

You can see the shed from the window in the new dining room, an extension built when some of the kitchen space was needed for a downstairs bedroom. Slowed down with angina, Damaris has built an alcove next to the kitchen just big enough for a single bed, a shelf for books and a radio — CBC music and news my preferences to this day, when I can find them — and a reading light on the wall above. There's a tiny bathroom across from it, also pink, cream and mauve, in what was an extra pantry. No need by then for more shelves to hold the overflow preserves and jams, "Now that I don't entertain as much," she says with a little smile. Whenever I ask how she is, she is crisp, "I'm managing," sometimes, "I'm managing just fine." No more discussion. Never an "organ recital," her term for boring, chronic medical complaints.

Even when she can no longer garden, Damaris is still pickling and needs help to shop for the ingredients. My daughter Hilary, making her own Cheltenham memories, takes Damaris in her wheelchair to the Orangeville Market to choose the perfect cucumbers for gherkins. They move from one vegetable stand to the next, Damaris eyeing the condition of that farmer's offerings. No simple task, they must be exactly the right colour, firmness and size. No substitutes, nothing second best.

Last of all the quilting frame takes its winter place in the dining room ready for the Cheltenham quilting bee to join the long woman-line of family seamstresses and fabric artists from earliest time. The women will make individual blocks to piece into the big quilt they're working on, or pieces to appliqué on an elaborately stitched background pattern. Week by week the design emerges, like a painting from an artist's brush. The women work collaboratively, talk, laugh and exchange the week's news as they sew. I look at the newly sketched patterns of this winter's quilt, know the skill that will make them, wonder what messages their colours and forms will shape.

Damaris has also been working on a dozen quilted bags in gorgeous colours and I ask if I may buy one. "Certainly not," she says with asperity. "They're going to the bazaar." Although not the crocheted throws of her younger years, for Damaris, the quick sale of the eagerly awaited bags brings satisfaction and comfort. She still makes beautiful things, is still a valued part of the community, with something to offer. To me, she herself is offering enough, but I am family and will always be there. *She gave me one that Christmas, presumably one that hadn't sold.*

Renewed by the comfort of Cheltenham's physical support, by the aunts' enduring love, which had not cracked for me during divorce, single parenthood, a troubled relationship with my sister, and illness, and from the distance of fifteen years and age 45, I can accept that frailty is a condition of being human. It is our humanness that drives us to "see only one," our feelings so fierce that they can cut us off from our other selves, our wholeness, our otherness. In retrospect, what had happened at Philip's death was like an explosion shattering the idylls of my childhood, and the unexamined optimism of my youthful heart and mind, of what the people in my life seemed to have been. I had so wanted the sisters' cruelty to my mother to be an aberration, as if they alone could shape their lives. As if their decisions were entirely individual, conscious, controlled. As if their behaviour were separate from the abusiveness, anger and sorrow — and the silence that surrounded it that drove the shaping influences of memory underground. I can never know the memories and feelings, or what engendered their overwhelming power, that erupted in their grief about Philip and spilled out to wound their sister. The dark side of their Presbyterian/Plymouth Brethren heritage that infused their family life with contradiction and sometime chaos, and the society that condoned and supported it was "bred in the bone."[9] And what is bred in the bone comes out in the flesh.[10]

If I thought about their troubled family past I had assumed, given what I knew of how they lived, that they had somehow come to terms with it in a way that enabled them to live contented and productive lives. Now the crater created by that explosion in me begins to fill with seeing, and understanding, how much less visible love is than strength. How, vulnerable to loss, love can twist into possessiveness and betrayal, hollowing our strength to a brittle skeleton. And survive that awful winter to grow new gardens. As we have.

THERE IS ALWAYS CHRISTMAS

Misty memories of a snowy Christmas Eve drive to Barrie in 1932, fresh-cut pine smells from the huge glittering tree in the hallway behind my grandparents at the open door; 1933, the year Damaris comes all the way to North Bay on the train. "Lucky to have a job," everyone said about Dad's Depression-era transfer in the coldest winter then on record. Dad had warned her to wear a hat or she'd freeze her ears. Damaris never wore hats. Her ears froze as she walked from taxi to front door — that sideways grin, and lift-of-her-eyes shrug!

Mother is the married daughter. In 1934, back from the "frozen north," our home in North Toronto is the place for birthdays and holiday gatherings: sisters cook, talk and laugh in the kitchen, "set out" the feast, Jane and I entertain visiting uncles and Dad's sister Cora. His oldest sister Maud lives in California, crippled with arthritis, and visits only in summer. He tends the fire, distributes gifts, pours drinks while we pass around the hors d'oeuvre. The table laden with covered dishes and everyone seated, the turkey is borne in, resplendent in white leg frills, dressing overflows the crop. Dad, beaming from the head of the table, "does the honours."

I inherited my mother's role, my daughters, mine. As I sit in their living rooms now, visiting with off-duty grandchildren and guests, the rise and fall of women's talk and the bursts of laughter

*from the kitchen echo down the years — of staircases, kitchens,
living rooms, women's voices.*

In 1975, when the drive from Cheltenham to Toronto in winter
becomes too much for Damaris, we go to Cheltenham on Boxing
Day. As usual, friends and family have come for Christmas Eve
supper and carol singing and I'd cooked dinner with all the
trimmings on Christmas Day. On the 26th it's time to read a
Christmas book and eat cold turkey sandwiches. But this is the
aunts' Christmas. "Enough family," mutter the children. But we
rouse early enough to arrive on time for lunch at 1:00. They have
been preparing for several days, will tire easily.

They are at the open door, the lighted tree behind them, drifting
hints of the meal to come. The tall cloth and cardboard wise men
rising over the manger scene they've made rest on cedar boughs
among fat beeswax candles on the fireplace mantel. The fire sparks
with pine cones, drinks are poured, presents opened and my still
lurking fears of someone breaking a precious piece of glass fade as
Damaris assures me, "You never broke anything when you were
a child. Why would they?" Has she forgotten the pickle dish? My
children say that they don't remember being afraid of breaking
anything — until they take their own children there.

Asparagus and egg casserole every year, with salad, their "own"
Parker House rolls, ice cream, "Grandmother's shortbread" with
the lemon icing, dark and light Christmas cake. One of us will
take a happy Rex, the latest King Charles spaniel, for a longer
walk than Damaris can manage. Others admire the winter quilt
in progress, a new piece of rose or amethyst glass, Getty's paper
dolls as they unfurl beneath the scissors. We leave three hours later
with tea cozies, knitted mitts and hats, jars of jam and preserves,
step out into the four o'clock shadows, "No, no you can't help
with the dishes, it's easier for us to do them." We have quietly
rinsed and stacked them during the afternoon. When will they do
them? They look so tired. "How do they do it?" I ask myself, as
everyone waves goodbye. "How does any woman do it?" Aware,
once again, of the long line of strong women stretching behind,
around and beside me.

Wherever the Christmas table is now, my mother's silver
candelabra take pride of place on the antique tablecloth, an

Aunt Getty tea cozy covers the teapot. Aunt Helen's paintings enliven our walls and Aunt Damaris's needlepoint hearth bench sits in front of my daughter's grate. Missing before dinner are the jewelled jars of layered fruits for Manhattans she made every year, her discussion with my father about the exact way to mix one. And the expression on her face, half indulgent, half dismay on the day my father offered me my first Manhattan....

GROWING OLD: THE 1980S

I don't remember when Getty had her first small strokes — she didn't mention them to us, only her good friend Gertrude Purcell knew and it was she who phoned me the summer of '91 to tell me Getty had called from London to say she wasn't well and asking me to meet her at the airport in Toronto. I'll never forget her face when she saw me — pain, bewilderment, relief and embarrassment that if I am there — she had never wanted me to meet her after her other trips — I must know something is up. Soon after, she moves to a small senior's apartment of eight units in Thornhill, just large enough for her drop-leaf dining room table with needlepoint cushioned chairs she had made and the Governor Winthrop desk whose three shelves hold treasures from her travels. The collection of tiny crystal perfume bottles glitters behind the glass shelves and I still smile in delight at the one I have, with a sense of poignancy too, at these small, very beautiful gestures of feminine frivolity from a woman of such simplicity.

After a while I notice that her memory isn't as sharp — she called her memory her "forgettery." I know she, not Damaris, is the only one who will talk about family history and ask her if she will let me record a few of the Rodgers stories. No point in asking for Beattie or personal stories. She "isn't comfortable" with the idea, but agrees. She begins with a little about her seafaring ancestor, an 1850s Fifeshire sailor, her visit to Menzies Castle, the ancestral home, and an astonishing meeting. In Perth a familiar-looking man came up to her and asked if she is a Rodgers. He is too! They have tea and a brief visit, just enough to establish the connection, before she has to leave. I never know if they corresponded because

Getty, who is looking more and more uneasy, suddenly says she must get ready for a bridge date with the other residents. I can never persuade her to talk about the details of the family's past, or her life, again. She is a bright woman and I suspect she knows that her forgettery already holds many of them.

Getty can no longer drive to Cheltenham. Jane or I drive her up whenever we can, not as often as we'd like, but Damaris always says, "I can manage, I don't need to put down so many preserves, people don't eat as much jam now as they used to."

John, a neighbour's son, has taken over cutting the grass and looks after the garden at Cedar Close as best he can when he's home from college. Weeds overgrow the corn hill, tomato plants and beans are planted in a smaller patch, sweet peas in pots are tended by neighbours and friends and by us.

But she begins to lose track of when she has taken her heart medication and the house is getting beyond her. Neighbour women are getting older too, afternoon bridge and sherry parties, even casual visits, drop off. Their absence makes me realize how essential they have been to Damaris's being able to stay at Cedar Close for as long as she has.

The 1990s

The clan gathers for a rousing ninetieth birthday party in the summer of 1990. Neighbour John outdoes himself and the perennial beds are a glory. Admiring guests wander in the garden, drinks in hand, my son Michael takes pictures, he says, to "help him remember forever." Collecting memories, as I am. Food from many kitchens overflows the tables, the speeches are fond, funny — and tearful. The four nieces are persuaded to wear dresses from the 1920s unearthed from village attics and to dance the Charleston, after hilarious lessons from Jane, me and a young neighbour, who can't resist dressing up too. The aunts keep time, are so delighted that I wonder when and where they learned to dance in the midst of full-time professions and the endless daily tasks of "making-do." Not in their pastor-ruled home for sure. Many more pictures are taken, a book will be made.

And then Cedar Close is on the market. I know the sale of the house will support Damaris for the rest of her years. Why is she so worried about money? Grace Elliot, who will be her executor, tells me that Damaris hadn't expected to live so long, is worried that she will "outlast her money," will not be able "to leave a little behind" — for us. (I know that worry, and that desire now.) And so she is torn: to sell or give away a lifetime's collection? The antique dealers hover, most of the rose glass and the willow-patterned china finds its way to their shelves, not much of it to those whose names — like Jane's — are stuck on bits of paper on the bottom. The once-given fire screen will not be "part of her will" and graces another hearth. Hurtful decisions swallowed, family and neighbours help her pack, unpack, repack and ignore the bursts of bad-temper and indecision that mask her wrenching despair at leaving her home of 50 years, and, inevitably, her hard-won independence.

There is tea and cookies in the seniors' residence that Damaris and her friend Grace Elliot have found not too far from the village and "pretty handy" for neighbours to call. Lunch can be "taken" if we call ahead. Afterwards we visit in her small sitting room, chat about village doings and current affairs. Damaris's mind and social connections are as up-to-date as her wardrobe and our discussions, usually political and never about religion or family, are always enriched by anecdotes about old friends, and the "goings-on" of the younger generations.

We leave with little gifts of unmarked china, which means it's old, or nineteenth-century pressed glass she has tucked away in the one closet in her apartment, saved so that she will always "have something for us." Sometimes I try to tell her how much she has given me down through the years. A nod, a little shrug, a deprecating smile and she changes the subject. Eventually I realize that the gifts are as complex as she is: beautiful, unique and practical, they are little "I love you's," small embodiments of her feelings and character. They also speak of her continuing need to make a contribution with something useful and beautiful. To be seen in a particular way, and with a reciprocity that means she is still part of family and community.

Soon after, Gertrude must move to Belmont House, a seniors' residence. The police had found her driving her car downtown at midnight. We visit her doctor. Getty turns to us, bewildered,

"How could I do that?" Acknowledges, "Well, if I did, of course I must move," and then her forgettery confronts us as she asks again, and again, and heartbreakingly again. "Why must I move? Where will I know to come home to?" We visit nursing homes and she hates all of them. Who doesn't? She and I are interviewed by the director of the Madison Ave. wing of Belmont House in Toronto, a former colleague of mine trying to be objective and professional, who agrees to admit her if she can be "oriented" in three weeks. Once more the family gathers and we are there every day until she knows her way around better than most of the other residents. There is a birthday party with family and her three good friends, residents also. Doris Walton plays the harmonica as merrily as she had at Getty's 75th. We watch for her tentative smile of recognition.

And then Damaris tells us she needs more care than can be provided at a seniors' residence for someone with congestive heart failure. No one says what kind of care this is and she is quick to reassure us, "I have seen them all, I will have the best of care." I imagine her, part imperious old woman, part experienced homemaker and wonderful cook, part eagle-eyed professional, inspecting what's available, knowing full well that she will make-do with what will be her last home.

She does just that. There is a ninety-second-year birthday party. Smiling staff bring small gifts to add to the family heap, eat cake, say, "We get such a kick out of your aunt. She's a wonder for her age, up to date with the news and always asking about our jobs and our families."

On our last visit, Damaris is temporarily in hospital for yet another lung drainage. After the procedure Jane and I, now in our sixties, stand by her bedside, daughter Hilary nearby. She looks very small, seems softer. Age and illness seem to have mellowed those sharp corners. She has told us that living in institutions is very much like living in a small village where she learned long ago, that to avoid hard feelings and to get along, "You never say anything about anyone to anybody." Age and illness also underscore that life-saving necessity. But those old eyes still blaze with tender pleasure, "Isn't it wonderful how well you've turned out."

My daughters, now in their fifties, laugh and ask, "Mom, have we turned out yet?"

At 93, Damaris wants no more hospital rescues from fluid-filled, heart-congested lungs. We have our instructions. When the call comes from the nursing home one late night she is released to die in peace.

We don't tell Gertrude that Damaris has died; there is a collective fear the news would be too upsetting. Because she forgets from moment to moment she would have to be told over and over again and that seems as if it would be a kind of torture. Will she really never know? When she must finally move to a protected floor of the nursing home the well-meaning staff tell her she no longer has any need for her keys, cane and purse. With Getty-like determination she has held on to these last signs of her independence, her particular brand of lady-like femininity and her life-long need for privacy and quiet. Gone, she no longer knows who she is or who we are. Her room door must always be open, "for her own safety." Her face is creased in worry. A nurse is concerned that she doesn't come to the afternoon gatherings, prefers to be on her own. "She always has," I reassure her. Hearing her "oh, oh oh" even before I see her, I ask the nurse if not knowing me means my visits are no comfort to her. "Oh yes," now she is reassuring me, "she is always happier after you have been with her." As am I.

Gertrude dies at 85 in July 1994, her brother Campbell in September, age 95, and Helen on Christmas morning, only 77. Jane has visited Helen in Kelowna, admired the wonderful gardens around her small house, met some of her friends, and spent hours in painter-talk, happy that Helen has finally come into her own as a painter. They spoke briefly of Philip's death, how there was concern that the bond between Philip and Grace might "take over," wanted time with him by themselves, misjudged the timing, said how that grievous error has haunted her all her life. Over the years Helen and I had segued into a comfortable long-distance friendship. Now I felt some satisfaction in Helen's acknowledgement of her error, but resolutely refused to entertain, for more than that one fleeting moment, any feelings of triumph. It would also have been a self-judgement.

My family is going to Jane's for the first Christmas dinner at her house for many years. When she opens the door, the familiar smells and sights of Christmas behind her, our "Merry Christmas" dies on our lips at her broken-up face, and her daughters, Anne and Sophie, hovering sorrowfully behind. Helen, true to form, has told us few details, just that she was being monitored for recurring tachycardia in hospital. She died there.

The turkey is cooked and must be eaten, gifts are opened, dishes done, the kitchen cleaned. We get through the day, hardly aware yet that they are all gone: grandparents, parents, aunts, uncles.

STANDING ON THE EDGE OF MEMORY

On a sunny day in June of '95, numb and reeling from my son John's death that April, Jane suggests a drive in the country. Somehow, we find our way to Cheltenham, stop the car on the road outside Cedar Close. New windows are huge, sightless eyes set uneasily in to the wide old boards. The side porch is enclosed — the clematis and climbing roses destroyed. We turn away from the rest and drive to the Elliot's. Grace holds us close in wordless hugs, gives us tea and cookies, tells us the kitchen and bathrooms are remodelled, the cellar floor tiled, the perennial beds reduced to a manageable size, the vegetable hill "gone to wild." She asks us to help her clear up some details. Damaris has left something for us.

Getty "put aside" from her modest salaries as secretary-treasurer to travel. Awestruck in the churches and cathedrals she visited she sent us letters about her adventures, left a small bequest. My mother travels after we're grown, writes journals we read after her death, wondering how she managed to leave us stories and "a little something." Although far away, Helen never fails to send us her lovely, poignant paintings of gardens for birthdays and at Christmas. I will travel with the money she and Damaris leave behind, "To spend on something frivolous," Damaris's last words instruct. Which means not on the children or the house, but on myself. Not a Plymouth Brethren value by a long stretch.

Now, from the perspective of a long life, and the long journey of coming to understand the stories that have shaped my life, I see that they must have understood full well the consequences of their upbringing. J.C. I "loved to cook and bang pots and pans around the kitchen," but he never welcomed his children there. Intent on keeping up appearances so that they will reflect well on him, he seemed not to reflect on what was good for them. He was given to unpredictable, fearful bursts of furious rage, was rejecting and critical of his children.

Margaret Beattie was their saving grace, a devoted mother who "understood children, and who talked to them" (G.E.C.'s letters). (*My heart swells at the image of her lying beside Jack to comfort and reassure him as he lay dying.*) Burdened with unremitting work and deep losses, she was constant, loving and strong throughout her marriage to an erratic and angry man. And gifted with children who helped her "live ten good years."

While almost never a subject of conversation, the aunts and my mother never denied this. Their lives were not lived on a constructed surface but on understanding what their parents' behaviour had meant to them — choosing to understand the badlands but live in greener pastures — whatever that was for each of them. As D. J. Spiegel says,[11] constructing an "earned secure" narrative from a mixed-messages, chaotic childhood is almost never possible without someone who is attuned to your feelings and needs, as their mother was to theirs.

Five brothers, cherished throughout their lives by each other and the women in the family, made their way as best they could. Only Campbell survived his sisters. The two who died so young, died of diseases that are treatable now. Two died in their prime. *Margaret Beattie's poignant conviction that George's addictions and erratic behaviour were due to "lack of mothering" is surely borne out by the work on child development since then.* And Philip's death, finally surrounded by loving sisters, highlights that no narrative is impenetrable, and that the life stories we live with can be violently disrupted by feelings and memories that burst through without warning from the depths of one's being.

Four sisters, loving, faith-filled deeds and doing, well-socialized Protestant introverts. They left so much more than "a little" behind. Their bleak, sorrowful sides were almost always as hidden and earthbound as the cellar floor at Cedar Close, sometimes schismed in a misjudged step when the light fails, and as illuminated as those glittering jars in basement cold rooms, replenished yearly by an interwoven web of independence, beauty and practicality. I know them, not via a persona or invented social self, but from the parts of their world they wished to share from the shadows that unbearably and unwittingly intruded. And I know them through all the ways they couldn't know about, by being themselves, faults and all. No substitutes.

I am thankful to them for giving me the childhood they did not have, for the loving sanctuary that opened up spaces for curiosity … to keep on digging … questioning, for my own understanding and peace … for the sake of my children, and their children. And for accepting that not all questions can be sufficiently answered.

All that and what I can't quite articulate, encapsulated at the end in a rose-painted china teacup, a penciled manuscript, a crystal perfume bottle, a painting of gardens … the struggle for words to say…

Travel Companions

The rose root from Scotland
generations of fences. Patterns
for tea cozies, quilted bags
        ribbons of dancers on door posts,
storied quilts — wedding flowers
        funeral wreaths.
A Nelly Moser clematis, birds
play in the tangled vines.
The recipe for Grandmother Beattie's
plum chutney lists ingredients only
        the rest is membership
in long meandering lines
of laughing, disputing
women who know what to do, is
        up to you to leave
a little behind, knowing

nature is birthplace, birthright
condition of existence
and survival.
Difference is surface deep
surfaces can be deep, resonating
	with sounds of silence sighing
over parched earth and deep pockets of pain
hide in awful simplification.
	A chilled emptiness of untold stories.

The radiance of the good
	illuminates all kinds of faces.
Beauty is in kindness and the everyday.
We are each other
	there is safety in numbers.
When body speaks, *do it now!*
Remorse is worse than grief.
Love grows in the fractures of our lives,
passion lies beneath words and
	wordlessness,
the heart is where home is, the soul
her sister.

ENDNOTES

---

[1]From the song "Weave and Mend" by Mary Trup. See end of book for lyrics.
[2]"Swing Low Sweet Chariot." First recorded in 1909 by the Fisk Jubilee Singers. "Pennies from Heaven," music by Arthur Johnston, lyrics by Johnny Burke. Introduced by Bing Crosby in 1936. "Good Night Irene." Origin unclear. First recorded by Huddie Ledbetter (Leadbelly) in 1933. "Red Sails in the Sunset," music by Hugh Wilkas, lyrics by Jimmy Kennedy. Published in 1935.
[3]Letters to Meggie by Grace Eunice Carson, unpublished.
[4]Letters to Meggie by Grace Eunice Carson, unpublished.
[5]Letters to Meggie by Grace Eunice Carson, unpublished. J.C.B. II, private correspondence.
[6]See "Beginnings" in *The Risks of Remembrance* (Toronto: Words Indeed, 2010), p. 69.
[7]Alistair MacLeod, "The Vastness of the Night" in *Island: The Collected Stories*. (Toronto: McClelland and Stewart, 2001).

[8]Quoted in Pam Bustin, "Ground: From Hanoi to Hiroshima in the Wake of 9/11," *The New Quarterly,* #121, Winter 2012

[9]"What's bred in the bone will not out of the flesh," old English proverb that serves as an epigraph to Robertson Davies' novel. *What's Bred in the Bone* (Toronto: Macmillan Company of Canada, 1985).

[10]The proverb rephrased by Laurie R. King, *The Moor* (New York: Bantam Books, 1998).

[11]D. J. Siegel, *The Developing Mind: How Relationships and the Brain Interact to Shape Who We Are* (New York: Guilford Press, 1999).

Border Lines
Loss and Redemption

Marilyn Walsh, "Chickadee," Wings and Wires series, 2008, Mixed media, etchings with embroidery, 6 x 4 inches.

Testing the Spirit

Ananias and Sapphira were members of a Christian community that held all property in common. Those who sold property or houses brought the proceeds of the sale and "put them at the feet of the apostles, and they were distributed to each according to need. There was no needy person among them. Ananias, with Sapphira his wife in agreement, sold a possession ... and kept back part of the price." (Ananias and Sapphira, Acts 5)

You were "privy to his plan," agreed
to keep a portion of the proceeds
promised to God
money for a poor crop, a rainy day?

I've done that, fudged the grocery money
a dollar here and there, every day
week by week —
for an emergency, a special dinner, new glasses,
a birthday gift for the one I love,
or to get ahead just enough to feel secure.

Or was it that God's law seemed unfair?
To give all to the church, thinking
"Could they miss so small a portion
who have so much compared to us?"

It is said that the heart

and mind of the community
beat as one. Was yours a promise
or an expectation? Given freely?

Or did women routinely go
along with husbands, who voted as God's
representatives in the earthly family,
assigning management of their commitment
to wives and daughters?

Your upraised arm in fear of
whose reprisal? His? the Neighbour's?
Your own foreknowledge
of the lies? Or did you see —
too late — that your lie alone would strike
a fatal blow?

Quilt Trails

Once in a while, along a country road,
painted wood or metal squares point
the way to a town-proud building,
a view that took an artist's breath away,
a mark for the last trace of a private death,
or vestige of a battle ground.

1811— Indians reveal a trail along a tract
of Carolinian Forest named *"the Longwoods,"*
widened to make a route for gun carriages
and a foot-path for men — aboriginal and white —
who will trudge to war.

Now, two hundred years later, women
living along The Longwoods Road
The Old King's Highway #2
record the war of 1812 another way.

"Broken Dishes," "Moravian Star," "Rail Fence,"
three patterns among 60 pieced blocks
stitched together in two quilts, each block
joined in a common border.

Detached quilt blocks will travel separate paths
to heritage barns between Thamesville
where Tecumseh lost his life and Delaware,

a British encampment, to show how
women and children lived the pain.

Herstorians delve archives
to write a story for each quilt block.
Sixty quilt blocks. Sixty stories.

In October my Aunt Damaris
brings the quilt frame indoors from the side porch,
sets it up in a corner of the dining room
for that winter's Circle Bee. Every quilt
is destined to be an heirloom, or sold at the bazaar.

I own one, appliquéd pink and mauve tulips
cupped by green leaves. Different patterns
for each of my children. Wedding gifts
to last lifetimes and beyond. The quilts
must be hand-stitched, no machine shortcuts allowed.

Damaris tells me the art of quilting evolved
from Ancient Egypt through the Middle Ages.
First as warm clothing and bedcoverings
and a bit of coloured gaiety peeking through
petticoats or bedskirts. Then art pieces,
tales of love* and battle stitched together.
Fabric troubadours telling our stories for centuries:

The quilt codes African-American slaves
used to follow the underground railway.**
"Tumbling Blocks" (get ready to go),
"Wagon Wheels" (pack for a long journey),
"Bear's Paw" (head north over the Appalachian Mountains).
Secret messages hung on lines in full view,
each a woman's spoor tracing freedom.

I remember the circle of quilters chortling
over the way his plaid shirt pieces were placed
to show he was a bad actor, "he plays around, take care"

murmuring over a khaki patch, pieces
of a child's dress, still new

Women stitching, laughing, news-making, grieving
Together. Quilts track history. Quilts in cloth, wood or metal
sign war routes, hidden foot-paths, ousted secrets, local beauty.
Proudly sold at church bazaars, high on a barn wall, or strung
along a country highway. Anyone who looks can learn the stories.

There will be 60 eight-foot-square murals on barns
along 65 kilometres of The Longwoods Road.
The Women's road of history for the war of 1812
tracks hidden paths into the present.

*The Tristan Quilt, 1395
**In *Hidden in Plain View: A Secret Story of Quilts and the Underground Railroad* by Jacqueline Tobin and Raymond Dobard (New York: Knopf Doubleday, 2000).

Coming of Age During WWII and Beyond

Young Children

1937. I was ten years old when WWII began, but my first memories of impending trouble began well before 1939. I suppose I was six or seven when my sister Jane, a year and a half younger, and I began to have dinner with our parents, rather than an earlier children's supper. A marker event — never mind that we couldn't talk nearly as much — and for several years a happy time, until I became aware of an undercurrent of tension. By 1938, dinner had to be over at seven o'clock, the dishes at least stacked in the kitchen so there would be no noise to interrupt the BBC news. The radio — no TV of course — was in the dining room and easy family conversation was silenced as we sat, glued to the thready, static-y, impeccably accented voice of the announcer. The "top of the news" stories (we picked up such terms at an early age) grew gloomier and gloomier and our parents' faces more serious and tense when Neville Chamberlain's speech, "Peace in Our Time" (after the Munich Agreement, Sept. '38) had no effect on Germany's invasion of Czechoslovakia's Sudetenland later that year in October. They had control of the entire country by March of '39 and the possibility, and then inevitability, of war came closer. It got to the point where I almost dreaded the dinner hour. After the news Jane and I did our homework at the dining room table, our parents' voices rising and falling in the next room, no longer the light "how was your day" chat but quiet, serious, murmuring to be interrupted with only the direst of homework emergencies.

The news got worse and worse. Poland was invaded in September 1939 and the Allies declared war.

1939. We were too young to understand what was happening or why it mattered when it was so far away. But children are never too young to soak in the atmosphere and live a sort of tentative parallel existence in the midst of adult worry, while being much more interested from day to day in what filled our lives. We were young enough that school was still interesting and a challenge, and for teachers to think that grim war news was not fit for young ears. But what made them think that we didn't know something was up? We would rather have known than live with uncertainty.

But it didn't seem all bad to us. Metal was in short supply, wrought iron fences were being torn up and shipped to factories so we happily denuded the closets of wire coat hangers so we could see the Saturday double bill with five cents and five hangers. Then all the hangers were made of wood or quilted cloth and we did errands to make the extra ten cents — and felt quite grown up.

My mother came from a long line of strong women and excellent cooks — her skills having been further honed in the privations of the depression — so we didn't much notice the rationing of meat, eggs, butter and cream. Except when she saved the butter ration for months so she could make a precious batch of real shortbread for Christmas. We made do with margarine, which came in a sickly off-white colour with a button of orange dye. It was fun to squish the dye in to the lardy substance but it turned such a ghastly neon-orange that we decided to leave well enough alone.

The only time I saw a whole pound of butter until well after the war was at my Aunt Damaris's weekend cottage when Jane and I went to visit her on the train on Friday afternoons. One August day we were invited to a corn roast and lo and behold we were told to roll our cob of corn in a pound of butter passed around on a china platter as if that happened every day. Corn, fresh-picked tomatoes, homemade bread with more butter and a seemingly unlimited supply of sliced ham ... it didn't get any better than that. And it certainly didn't. Of course we were very embarrassed to appear in public on the way home on Sunday afternoon with six-quart baskets of vegetables, four eggs per basket carefully wrapped and placed underneath them.

1940. Women had not been permitted to teach after they married; they'd be taking a job away from a man. But since many of the male teachers were in the armed forces women could take their place, temporarily, and my mother was allowed to teach again.

Women were also needed to work in munitions factories, restaurants and even fire departments. Often just teenagers, they worked ten hours a day, six days a week and could even appear in public wearing "slacks" — which greatly impressed my sister and me.

As it was for the factory workers, the money was a welcome addition to our family finances, but there was no doubt at all that my mother was very happy to be back in the classroom. She was an honours university graduate in history and English. Loved books. Loved to teach. Each day was a new challenge for her and she was in her element — and was usually home a few minutes after we were to fulfill her "womanly duties": housework was relegated to evenings and weekends and Jane and I were given extra chores to pick up the slack. When we complained we were told briskly to think of the children in war-torn Europe who had much less to eat and a much tougher life than we did.

That stopped us for sure because by now the German army seemed to spread across Europe like a plague, the news increasingly fearful. In May of 1940, France was invaded, the "invincible" Maginot line was bypassed, as if it was of no importance at all. The Allies were defeated at Dunkirk in June of 1940 … the sound of Churchill growling defiantly in his "We Shall Fight on the Beaches" speech rang through the house *and is still etched in my memory*. The Battle of Britain raged from July–September 1940. The dreadful London Blitz began in September, France fell and Vichy France was established in now-occupied German territory in the fall of that year.

There was daily news of ships and submarines destroyed or sunk and the incessant bombings in Britain. I was horrified to hear that very young children were evacuated from the major cities to the country to live with people they didn't know. Photographs of the new Queen Elizabeth, consort to King George VI, talking with exhausted-looking people among the bombed out buildings, began to bring home to us what the war meant to ordinary people. The fate of European Jews was just beginning to filter into the public press. But the political decision in 1939, which would become a national shame, to forbid 907 Jewish refugees on board the ship St. Louis to land, didn't make it into the news until much later. "None is too many," an immigration agent said of Jews such as those on the St. Louis. Turned away, the ship made for Belgium. Weeks later the French rounded up the Jews and sent them to concentration camps. As Hitler's forces marched across Europe and bombarded the British Isles there were very real, daily fears that the Allies might lose the war and Britain too would be occupied. What would this mean for us? Air raid practices with sirens shrieking and moaning became a part of everyday life, pamphlets advising what food to store and for how long were kept under the front cover of the recipe book.

It is hard to remember, even for those of us who lived then, how different Canada was 70 years ago. "Multicultural" was an unfamiliar term, many peoples' roots in Britain were very deep and there were few who did not have a relative there. As well, there were Canadians of many different nationalities who lived in fear of what was happening to their families — especially the Jews — in occupied Europe. And what happened to our own "Canadian" German and Japanese citizens is a shameful story.

"None is Too Many" is the title of the memorial in Halifax Harbour, designed by Daniel Libeskind, and placed 70 years later where the ship would have docked.

Growing into Adolescence

1941. Doing "your bit" became a priority. I sang in our high school choir on the steps of Toronto's City Hall, shivering with cold (school uniforms a must), in one of the war victory bond drives. We gave up our car after gas rationing took hold, went on our annual two-week summer holiday by train, walked wherever we could, or took a bus — your timing had to be perfect to catch fewer buses with schedules stretched out to save fuel. It was a long trek to the North Toronto Market, but if Mrs. McDonald's cream separator had broken down again it was worth it to buy four ounces of cream so thick you could stand a spoon in it.

And you could sometimes buy rabbit. Rabbit! I couldn't choke it down: shades of Flopsy, Mopsy and Cottontail.

And then we learned to knit. "Pre-teens" had not been invented yet, but learning to knit was a rite of passage among the women in our family — known for their needlework and quilting skills — talents that seem to have bypassed me. Not yet for us the fingerless gloves or balaclava hoods, but oh the triumph of knitting a mitt with a thumb, and then being able to turn the heel of a sock. We sat with other young girls, proudly no longer children, in a corner of the room where the churchwomen gathered weekly to knit, sew and pack boxes. Shared milky tea and biscuits. Listened to the talk. We were knitting for the "boys overseas" — British, Irish, Scottish — and then our own, as "colonials" enlisted and went "over there" to fight. Soon there were women and girls in the room whose husbands, fathers, fiancés had shipped out and the songs we heard on newsreels and radio like, "Over There," "Now is the Hour," "When Johnny Comes Marching Home" took on new meaning.[1] *The sentimental, false gaiety and false optimism of these songs still haunts me on Remembrance Day.*

South on Avenue Rd. from St. Clements Ave., where we lived at the end of the street there was an air force training base, part of the Commonwealth Air Training Program. Flight training was north of the city. Two or three airmen came for dinner every Sunday. They cleaned their plates of beef. I was young enough to harbour a small resentment that they were happily consuming the week's beef ration, old enough to know better than to say so. Or there would be chicken — and even rabbit. Whatever the menu, it was more than they could get at home, and much better than institutional cooking, so while they waited politely for the offer they always accepted seconds. Whole pies disappeared in minutes (apple and peach fillings from preserves in the cellar cold room) with a rare cup of coffee.

Stirred by emerging hormones, I was awed by their glamour: they came from cities, towns and villages with strange names, spoke with a variety of hard to understand accents. Mom and Dad were good at easing their shyness and as they relaxed they told stories of home: moms, dads, sisters, brothers, girlfriends — most of them were too young to be married or have children. My sister and I were way too young — and too closely supervised — to go dancing (we were not allowed to date until we were past 16) and so we listened enviously to casual references to dancing at the Palais Royale, and other places in the west end which seemed like the ends of the earth from where we lived in North Toronto. As the war went on they seemed like extended family, sort of like big brother substitutes and their parents often wrote letters to mine, thanking them for giving their sons "a home away from home."

Training completed they went back to fly Bombers or Spitfires. *When I look at photos of those small, fragile planes now, boy faces smiling from the cockpits, scarves jaunty around still-thin necks, I wondered how they — plane and boy — lasted as long as they did. Which wasn't likely to be very long — 922 British aircraft were destroyed during the battle of Britain alone (1,767 German).*

Soon other letters came from those parents telling us that Charlie, Joe, Rupert, Doug was missing in action, killed in action, a prisoner of war. The war became an immediate dark presence as I added a sentence or two to mother's letters of sadness, sympathy and offered prayers.

And then letters came that made the war much closer to home, a part of our personal lives. Uncle Philip, mother's brother and a chaplain in the air force, wrote to tell us that his fiancé, an air force driver, had been killed when her vehicle was strafed on the road. He never married. When mother read letters from her youngest sister Helen, an occupational therapist in the army, her voice quavered at the descriptions of injuries sustained not only by the military but also by civilians wounded in the relentless bombings of cities, towns and countryside.

One of their closest friends, an army engineer, had survived Dunkirk. Engineers were the first off the landing craft to prepare for the wave of soldiers coming ashore amidst heavy fire. And we were well aware that they were the first to die or be injured. One time when he was on leave he came for a very special, welcome-home dinner and could eat only a fraction of it, his system unused to what to us was an ordinary — although rationed — helping of meat. A few weeks later his wife Esme wrote to tell us he had been seriously injured when a piece of a bombed out building fell on him as he walked along a London street. It was so ironic as to be almost funny that he would survive Dunkirk and be felled by a chunk of cement, but she told us that many people were injured in the same way every day.

The gap between what we knew from the press and what was really happening was brought home to us by stories like these. No one had ever talked about why the troops would need the extra warm clothing we were knitting. Now we realized that no one said much about what the war must truly feel like for the people enduring the bombings, or the men fighting "at the front." We in Canada or the United States couldn't know about bomb-levelled streets or the horrors of combat when there were few images to tell us about them. Wartime news and propaganda focused on the bravery of the troops, or tried to strike a positive note. Like the caption of that famous photo of Queen Elizabeth talking and laughing with a group of women in downtown bombed-out London which read: "Despite their suffering, crowds smile happily when the Queen stops to chat with an East End mother and child during a tour of the Royal Family through this devastated area." There was no picture of the devastated area, and we only heard conversations heavy with innuendo, to convey the sense that more was being said than what was heard, or seen. I grew into a teenager wondering what was happening to ordinary people like me, my sister, my parents, the relatives of the Polish family down the street. *Questions that initially may have been the result of the self-absorption of adolescence, but these questions were to stay with me for the rest of my life.*

The U.S. had entered the war December 7, 1941 after Pearl Harbor but hopes of an early end to the war sagged with the invasion of Russia in June of '41 followed by the horrendous 900-day siege of Leningrad until 1943. The extent of the deaths from starvation and cold was literally indescribable. *When I was there a few years ago there were photographs in the front entrances of every museum, art gallery and public institution of what that place had looked like during the siege. The destruction, suffering and deaths of thousands of people in unforgettable images are still very present for the people living there today.*

Mostly we carried on with our own lives, as people do. For

us, the war was like a serial story that we listened to every day. Some chapters had concrete personal connections to our daily lives, like the tragedy of hearing of someone's loss, or of losing someone close to us — that left a hole, but we somehow learned to live around it.

1942–45. My parents worked, volunteer war efforts continued and Jane and I earned money at a series of progressively more grown up jobs: baby sitters, garden helpers, kitchen help at the T. Eaton Co.'s summer retreat for their staff (thanks to a nudge from Dad who worked at Eaton's), ward-aids (i.e., cleaners) at the old Sick Children's Hospital.

The Allies invaded Normandy on June 6, 1944 (*Operation Overlord*), and began the Liberation of Holland in September. Stalin, Churchill and Roosevelt knew the Germans were defeated and met at Yalta to set up demarcation lines between their armies February 4–11, 1945. The seemingly endless war ended on May 10, 1945.

People all over Europe struggled to rebuild, lived with rationing for many years after the war, in Britain until 1954; tried to live with — or to forget — their memories. *The Berlin Wall started going up in 1961 to prevent Germans from entering the West-controlled portion of the city, and fell in 1989.*

The war had begun for me with a personal marker event — being invited to the dinner table to begin to learn how to be an adult ... including the piling up of war images and questions that came with that transition. It ended at the same time as my first away-from-home job the summer of 1945. At sixteen, any student who achieved straight As in the spring exams qualified to skip the finals and work from the May 24th weekend to the end of the August harvest in the Niagara Region vegetable farms and fruit orchards. We lived in crowded dorms, ate dreadful food, worked from dawn 'til dusk for low piecework wages, and thought it was wonderful because we were on our own and parent-free for the first time.

Adult Years

1946. University, marriage, children, single parenthood, post graduate studies, career — with a little writing in between the cracks — occupied my adult life. I read a few books by post-war armchair strategists and books about battle and battlefields. Stories written by soldiers, airmen and sailors came many years later because the soldiers in Europe didn't tell their families about the conditions they lived and fought in. In the early years of the war the boys who enlisted, some as young as fourteen, who looked older because they were big, strapping western farm boy, told their parents they were eager to get over there before the "fun" was over. When they did get "over there," they didn't write home about it. Or talk about it when and if they came home. How could you tell your mother, then or later, that it was much worse than she'd feared it might be? Than she could ever have imagined? And so it almost looked as if they were having fun in their photos of picnics and of reading newspapers in fortified trenches that they sent home with their cheery letters of camaraderie, and jokes about the food not being as good as Mom's. How could anyone at home know how it really was for them? Or how they felt? Later in the war the propaganda posters showed determined looking men and smiling women, healthy and unmaimed, urging enlistment NOW! And those sentimental songs!

It wasn't until many years later, when people began writing about the conditions of living and fighting the war, rather than the wisdom, or stupidity, of the strategies of those in command, that the full enormity of *fighting* a war came home to those who had never been there.[2] But my questions about ordinary peoples' *experiences* during the war — civilians, especially women and children — went unanswered, although they were kept alive by occasional first-hand accounts and a series of vivid images.

One of my best friends at university, who had been a child participant in the Dutch Resistance carrying letters in a basket under heaps of tulips, which they ate, cooked; uncooked they were poisonous, told me a little of their dangers and privations — they were often starving — and of their joyous relief when they were freed by Canadian troops (September 1944).

Years later, I witnessed the continuing grief of the survivors of occupation. Ruth and I kept in touch after she returned to Holland, and I visited her several times. One year, I stood with a group of those survivors on the anniversary of VE day, clustered around the statue of a child commemorating all the children in that neighbourhood who had been shot in reprisal for their parents' participation in the resistance. On that day the statues are always covered in flowers. Some of the people gathered there were relatives, even grandparents of those executed children, sheets of tears covering their faces as a bugle played a lament. That was real, and not sentimental in the least. There were similar quiet gatherings and flower-heaped statues in every square in Amsterdam. In Canada there are memorials to the men and women who lost their lives fighting. As there should be. Public statues; paintings now rarely seen. As for civilian accounts: private photograph albums, a few published memoirs, and letters to "the boys" overseas on thin blue airmail paper.

In the late 1970s and '80s, many of the children of Holocaust survivors came to the counselling centre at York University where I worked. They wrestled with how to be the high achieving example their parents needed to justify their survival when their entire village had been wiped out. I realized I had no experience and scant resources to help them and I took a course with a psychiatrist who was himself a Holocaust survivor and parent of a child dealing with how her father's experiences were a part of her life.

And there was the story one of my clients told me years later in my private psychotherapy practice. She and her younger sisters and brother had been evacuated from London to the country during the worst of the Battle of Britain, as so many children were. She was the oldest, in charge of the young ones, and did her best to see that they were happy. Because of the constant and random bombings and of gasoline shortages, her parents could not visit them for more than a year. Finally they secured two of the precious places on a bus, and the children waited, ecstatic with anticipation. And waited. The bus never came. Days later they heard that the bus had been hit, all passengers killed. Life went on, my client grew up, married, immigrated to Canada, raised a family. She came to see me because of an increasing uneasiness which she could not explain. For months we worked with watercolour and clay and her slowly dawning realization that she had been looking for her parents all of her adolescent and adult life.

In the late 1980s, I was interviewing people for a graduate research paper. One of them told me a little of his wartime experiences. There was one image which struck home deeply for me.

He told me how he had seen a woman polishing the one window remaining in a bombed-out building in Europe when he was in the U.S. armed forces during the Second World War. Meyer tells me that to this day he can still hear the squeak of the rag, see her eyes staring ahead, not looking at the marching troops or the tanks rolling by. And continued:

> Why was she doing that? The building was wrecked; no one could live there. It seemed useless, but she was trying to make some meaning out of her life by doing something familiar. The war was over, she was free. We gave the kids candy, but it made them sick, just like the canned meat we gave the parents. They wanted it, but they couldn't eat it; it was too rich, they'd had nothing like it for years. There we were, the big liberators, feeling good and they were cheering us. We knew nothing. We thought they would be happy and that would be it. But where were they going to live? Where would they find food? Even cook it? We didn't think of that. It came right down to their daily life and what that meant and how much we didn't know about any of it, about what they'd been through and would go through for years. We had no understanding of that. We were too caught up in being victors. How could we know, coming from a country that hadn't had a war in hundreds of years? From then on, all of my life has been a search for meaning, in my own mind, in reading, in listening, in any way I can.[3]

Looking back now I realize that my "come and go" questions about the pervasive effects of war on ordinary people begun in my early years formed the foundation of my social-political perspective and my lifelong advocacy for social justice. Asking questions, looking in various literatures, listening to stories for rarely found answers about women and children steered me towards feminism, and rooted me there. Whose stories are told? Whose stories are recorded so they will be remembered?

There are monuments to those in uniform who had died fighting. Of course. I hope there are others, but in my not very extensive travels I saw few to civilians: the children in Amsterdam's squares, a monument to a sailor's wife waiting for his return in a Dutch port. There are many, many books and films about battles, battlefields and warriors. What about the nameless woman who Meyer saw? Who tells her story and the stories of the thousands and thousands like her about WWI and II? About any war? About the wars happening right now?[4]

Serendipity is amazing. Before I came to Manitoulin Island the summer of 2011, I helped to organize Salon 3x3, an event on October 30 in Toronto, with three poets and three painters riffing off each other's work in an informal coffee house setting. One of the painters, a United Church minister, had painted portraits of how she imagined some of the women in the Old and New Testament might look. I wrote a short poem about a nameless woman from the Old Testament:

No Name Women (Judges 11: 30–40)

Jephtha's daughter has no name.

Hot for battle Jephtha made a deal with God:
in return for victory he vowed to make a burnt
offering of "whatsoever" came
to meet him when he returned home
from the defeat of the Ammon, enemy to Israel.

His daughter and only child was the first
to greet him at his door with "timbrels and dances."
Thou, said Jephtha
"hast brought me very low and art one of them
that troubles me. I have opened my mouth
unto the Lord and I cannot go back."

Jephtha's daughter has no name.
A what. A trouble to him as he rent his clothes,
crying "Alas." She, not his vow, brought him low?
His word for her life.
She accepted that his promise to
the Lord meant death, asked only for two months
to wander the mountains "bewailing her virginity."

She "knew no man," left no issue to continue
his lineage? The Old Testament leaves us
to guess. And to question
men in wars who kill women, their children,
rape, pillage homes. Endless numbers,
centuries long disposable what-so-evers.

Women robbed of names.

Their homes burnt offerings to whom? Their
indiscriminate violation leaves nameless
seed exchanged for what vow?
Who amongst us accepts this on their behalf?

"It was a custom that the daughters of Israel went yearly
to lament the death of the daughter of Jephtha
four days in a year."

Nameless women bewail nameless daughters every day.

ENDNOTES

[1]"We'll Meet Again," words and music by Ross Parker and Hughie Charles, 1939. "There'll Be Bluebirds Over the White Cliffs of Dover," Jimmy Dorsey, 1942. "Comin' in on a Wing and a Prayer," The Song Spinners, 1943.
[2]Titles of several contemporary or well-known books about the horrors of WWII from the soldiers' point of view: Markus Zusak, *The Book Thief* (New York: Knopf, 2005); Otto H. Frank and Mirjam Pressler, editors, *The Diary of Anne*

Frank, translated by Susan Massotty. (New York: Doubleday & Company, 1952); Max Hastings, *Overlord: D-Day and the Battle for Normandy* (London: Simon and Schuster, 1984); *Max Hastings, All Hell Let Loose: The World at War, 1939–1945* (London: HarperPress, 2011); John Keegan, *The Second World War* (Toronto: Penguin Canada, reprint edition, 2005); Spencer Dunmore, *Above and Beyond: The Canadians' War in the Air, 1939–45* (Toronto: McClelland & Stewart, 1996); Blake Heathcote, *Testaments of Honour: Personal Histories of Canada's War Veterans* (Toronto: Doubleday Canada, 2002).

[3]Meyer's story is one of twelve in my book, *We All Become Stories: A Conversation with Twelve People About Their Experiences of Aging and Memory* (Cobourg: Blue Denim Press, 2013), p. 43.

[4]Recently noted in *GameSpot: This War of Mine, News & Features*, by Carolyn Petit, March 24, 2014. "Pawel Miechowski of 11 Bit Studios wants his upcoming game, This War of Mine, to challenge the way that games typically portray war by presenting it from the perspective of civilians who must survive from day to day in a war-torn city." Web.

Necessary Housekeeping

There is no love so pure that can survive without its incarnations.

—Michele Murray[1]

HIS GRAVE IS AT THE TOP OF A LITTLE HILL, TUCKED IN AT THE foot of his best friend's grave. I planted pansies there in the early spring and came back a month later to see how they were doing.

I parked the car at the bottom of the hill, my usual spot. The gravestones are flat, invisible until you're almost upon them, but from a distance you can see the colour of flowers saying hello. No hello this time. I climbed past the other graves: Sutton, Grover, McMichael, Baxter, the Salvation Army captains, friends now as I passed them. The little red flag that meant "special care" was planted near the grave, but the ground was dry and the pansies shrivelled.

A curly-haired young man was clipping grass around a new grave and I asked him if watering was included in special care. He assured me it was and we walked back, looked down at the desiccated pansies.

"It doesn't look as if these were watered recently."

He was silent for awhile.

"Maybe you should get new flowers."

"Mmn ... not much point, unless they're watered."

"Well you see, I'll tell you. I water them, sure I do, but the earth here and here, it's all mounded up, and the water just falls away and doesn't stay for the flowers."

"Could you maybe level the earth out a little?"

"Sure I could. You bring some new flowers and I'll plant them for you."

"Why, that's really nice of you. But you see, I'm going away in a few days and I'm pretty sure I won't have time to do that for awhile."

"Okay, I buy you some flowers. What do you like for here?"

Not knowing whether he knew the names of flowers in English we walked over to another grave so I could show him the fibrous begonias planted there. We agreed that these would do well in a dry, shady place. I asked him how much he thought it would cost and he shrugged away my question. I gave him 20 dollars "to start"; he smiled, and shrugged again, and assured me that when I came back everything would be "very nice." His name was Tony and I gave him my name as well.

Driving under the tree branches hanging over the curving roads of the cemetery I said hello to Mom and Dad as I passed their grave place. If you look fast you can see their stones from the Davisville station of the Yonge St. subway, just before the gate from the cemetery into the street. I was smiling to myself, a little incredulous that I had handed money to a stranger and trusted him to do what he said he'd do, then gave a mental shrug, and smiled again at how like his shrug my inner gesture was.

As it happened I had to go up north again for an emergency dental appointment the day before I was to leave and was curious to see if anything had been done. As soon as I got out of the car I saw colour. My heart beat a little faster.

I looked down, astonished. It wasn't just that the soil had been levelled and there were flowers. The tiny flowerbed around the grave, small enough to escape the notice of anyone who wasn't looking carefully, that little forbidden space, was edged in dark red brick. Not all of it discreetly dug into the soil, but punctuated with upended bricks at the corners and in the middle. There were red and pink fibrous begonias and blue ageratum in profusion. Well watered.

"You like it?"

Tony was beaming, a little anxious, but his face said, "How could you not like it?"

I loved it, and told him so. I loved it so much I couldn't stop smiling. And I knew that John would have loved it, would have joined in my delight, laughing. Would have known that I would be almost crying, and why: the little patch was unmistakably Italian, a miniature of the gardens in the downtown Toronto Italian neighbourhood he'd lived in, where he'd helped his landlady with the grapes and tomatoes and peppers. And tended the outdoor shrine to the Virgin Mary.

But I was worried there might be a problem and didn't know what to say without hurting Tony's feelings. He could be reprimanded for breaking the rules — it was certainly against the cemetery rules — and he might have to dismantle his carefully made little garden. He must have caught my thoughts because he frowned a little and asked me again:

"You like it?"

"Oh Tony I do, I really do."

"The guys they like it, they say I do a really good job."

"You did a wonderful job. It's beautiful. It's like a flower bed now, the gravestone looks just right against the brick, and the flowers show up well."

He looked relieved, "So it's all right?"

"It is, but you know, we may have a little bit of a problem."

"Why, what problem?"

"Well, you see the people who manage the cemetery, they may not approve. I'm not supposed to put much here, just something small."

"Okay. So we won't show them."

"Well ... there's something else. The person who has that grave" — I gestured to the stone above my son's — "she might be a little upset."

"But why? This is your family's grave."

"Well, not quite."

And I found myself telling him the story. He deserved to know at least the bare bones, about the two little boys who were best friends all their lives. *They played together every day, ran away from school when they were just little, found in the park so tired they could scarcely walk, weekends at the cottage learning to swim and paddle and sail, the firecracker accident that hurt his friend so badly, went on their first date together, lied through*

big smiles about drugs and drinking — and a whole lot else I
guess — talked every day on the phone until....

"His friend, John, died when he was nineteen, in a car accident,"
on Halloween night in the rain another car hit him as he was
reaching in the trunk to get the spare to fix a flat "and was buried
there, in that grave, just above this one."

My John stayed at the grave until after everyone had gone
down the hill. I looked back; he was throwing a handful of
dirt on the coffin as it sat above ground. Putting the coffin in
the ground was supposed to be too upsetting for everyone, as
if people weren't already 'upset.' Ravaged. The groundsmen
did that later, when the mourners had gone, but he wanted his
friend covered, he seemed so exposed, so   unfinished   it's
never <u>*finished*</u>*....*

"My son, his friend, came to the cemetery often, sat there among
the trees on the rise just above the grave, smoked a cigarette,
talked to his friend and shared his problems with him all those
years, as he'd always done."

Sometimes we'd visit his friend's grave together and afterwards
walk in the cemetery along the winding paths through gardens
and trees (he was a gardener himself) down to the ravine. Turning
back he'd comment on a grave marker he liked, "I walk here
often, it's a lovely place to be quiet in."

Sometimes we'd walk all the way over to where his grandparents
are buried. He loved them so much, was so distraught when they
died ... his look of desolation when his friend died, "You lose
everyone that matters."

"Seventeen years after his friend's death, my son died."

My John, by his own hand, shot through the head with one of
his father's guns, given to him as his part of the estate after his
father died, lying in the back of his van all emptied of tools and
clean and ready, so carefully planned ahead   in the head   how
long had he....

"We knew he would have wanted to be buried close to his
friend."

A few weeks before he died he and a friend, the other one of the
threesome, visited the grave and John said, so casually, "Here is
where I'd like to be buried some day, right here."

Then he took his friend down the road to look at a grave marker he liked, "Wouldn't it be great to have one like that?"

His friend told me he never guessed John could be planning his own death, wanted his friends to know what he'd like   he told me at the funeral   oh why didn't he tell someone earlier   maybe someone could have   could anyone have....

"His friend's mother agreed, said he could be buried at the foot of her son's grave."

We haven't seen much of each other since ... I've wondered if she felt she had a choice.

"And the cemetery management gave permission ... as long as the new grave wasn't too noticeable. So you see Tony, if they don't approve maybe you could take the upright bricks and lay them down, that way you really can't see anything except the flowers until you're right here. And you could say it helps when you cut the grass. The flowers will always show."

"In the winter maybe some berries, you know that bush?"

"You mean holly? That would be lovely."

"But *you* like it?"

"I love it. And if no one says anything we'll leave it just the way it is."

"Good. I wanted to make it beautiful for you. Like a little shrine."

"Well it is. That's just what it is. My son would know, he would like it here."

When I asked him how he'd found the time he told me he'd worked at it on his own over the weekend.

"I'd like to pay you for your time and for the extra flowers you planted."

"No, no the flowers were just $20. Besides I don't want the guys to see that you know because...."

They'd know that he was moonlighting, breaking the rules.

I held his arm as we walked down the hill to my car. "The grass is slippery and I don't want to risk falling." I rolled the window down, chatting, and put folded bills in his hand as he leaned against the car. He smiled again, "I'm glad you like it. I wanted to make it beautiful for you."

Going on my way along the winding roads we'd walked so

often, I smile and cry as I often do when I think of him. Years now? Ready to leave because I feel comforted. We are both looked after.

My family has grieved in our different ways, some still too raw to share memories. But I tell them about Tony and the flowers. In the fall, my older daughter and I climb the hill. The brick edging the flowerbed around the grave is still there, upright ones a little lumpy, already look as if they'd been there for a long time. The begonias and ageratum are frostbitten; the fallen autumn leaves around the stone marker have been swept to one side. As I clean away the remnants of summer my daughter plants a holly bush. Later, she returns to plant scilla bulbs to bloom in the spring.

ENDNOTES

---

[1]Murray quoted in Marilyn Sewell, ed., *Cries of the Spirit: A Celebration of Women's Spirituality* (Boston: Beacon Press, 1991), p. 88.

Again

There are days
when time has no other side but now,
when was, not decently

retrospective, fills my mouth,
chokes me with presences that
should be memories, not tastes.

"So long ago" they say.

I wanted him to keep on walking, even
when the ground fell away under him,
wanted him to find another voyage
so he could keep on living, so

there would be something else*
"But living killed him," I say.

There's nothing else.

*From Tennessee Williams, *Camino Real*, "Make voyages, attempt them.
There's nothing else."

Birds of a Feather

High overhead, flying silently in loose layers
the crows converge on the morning city. Hundreds
fan out in search of food, settle noisily
in lines of trees, nest here and there, leave, return,
swoop down to peck holes through garbage bags
then wheel away

to another site as the Food Bank doors open.
Quiet groups of women, men and small children
sort quickly through piled rows
of cans and packages, alert for apples,
oranges and day-old greens delivered
from last night's restaurant tables.

A huge cauldron of crows gathers in late afternoon,
balloons as the sun veers towards setting. Black thousands
cloud the sky, obscure treetops, somersault in play, flirt,
talk in grating caws and strange Krrrrr's, scare
the song birds, mess the ground, annoy the neighbours,
huddle together on dark winter nights

when they return to roost
and city shelters beckon. Gathered loungers
drift towards the day's meal eaten
at communal tables. Sporadic talk, then

in the dormitory curled around a few
possessions far away from bed bugs
and each other as space permits.

Ice Storm

Ice Storm 1: Toronto, December 21st, Watching and Waiting

Christmas has been difficult since John died. The only one of my four with no children, we'd go together to choose a tree, put it up, string the lights and leave it to thaw until the next night when he and Helene would come over. We'd lovingly unpack the boxes of ornaments, some generations old, decorate the tree, douse the house lights, kindle a fire ... candles, sandwiches and scotch, mince pies, listen to the angel chimes go 'round ...

Just because a bad storm is forecast isn't a good enough reason to give up a pre-Christmas celebration with an old friend. So we don't give a lot of thought to freezing rain, then more snow for the next 24 hours, other than to make excuses: the evening planned for weeks, hard to find another night so close to Christmas, Steve could take a cab. There will be few cabs for days. But we agree to meet earlier in case the weather gets really serious.

We have a lovely time: a favourite restaurant, great food, good talk. Oblivious to the increasing clatter of hard rain rattling the windows we linger on to enjoy the three-piece Greek band, and the spontaneous dancing from several other tables. So mellow and happy — until the door bangs open and a shivering group of four bursts through, frozen-faced and soaking wet.

Hurriedly we bundle up. Chef Lambros hovers over us, stands tall in the doorway watching Steve help me over the now ice-crunchy snowbank safely into my car. Watches as Steve makes his slow, limping way across the already treacherous street to the subway station.

Little fingertips of sleet scratch the car windows, but a clear road west until Southwood (south of the woods in yesteryear). Downhill the road slicks, tires judder, veer sideways; I'm getting nervous — want to be home before the entire road ices over. Curve left and south again, slowly slip-slide along the driveway into the parking lot for our row of houses. Worry flares again — no nighttime glare from tall poles illuminates the bleared yellow lines dividing proper car places. No Christmas lights on the backyard tree in the neighbour house to the north. "Ahh" ... our houses and coloured lights glimmer in the shadows. A gingerly foot out the car door slides away on an invisible sheet of ice. Put icers on my boot soles (stored in the glove compartment), a clumsy manoeuvre with my injured left leg, reach for the extra cane, mutter encouraging words as I nerve myself to venture forth.

A voice in the shadows calls out. Carefully navigating his way to the utility house with boxes and scraps from Christmas wrappings, my neighbour says, "Wait a minute Ann, I'll put this in the garbage — let me walk you to your door." Arm in arm, canes assisting on either side, we creep slowly along the walkway past the half-walls on our right, red brick new bright under their ice-coated surface. Oak tree branches from the near neighbours' tree bend alarmingly low over the high fence to our left, scrape the walkway, graze my arm as we pass, each clacking leaf stiff in its icy frame. Encased in glittering silver, bare twigs of vines and shrubs, like tiny skeleton bones under see-through flesh, sway on the house walls, the hairy seedpods on the clematis shiver a sudden gold over them all.

We reach my patio gate, flung wide in wind-clamour, greeted inside by the wildly swinging bird feeder. Lights glint in the honeysuckle vine, still surprisingly in leaf, and on the holly bush, each leaf and berry a frozen morsel. Pale stone goddess sheened silver, bird bath topped in glossy black ice, pots of small, pale green cypress trees circled in shiny ivy and glazed red apples standing frozen on either side of the green door, its brass fittings glitter as if newly burnished. Home.

"*Thank* you."

"Anytime ... just call."

Warming my hands around a mug of steeping tea, feet on the jacked up baseboard radiator in the kitchen, I listen to the news; hurriedly unbox the wind-up radio stored on a shelf in the front hall cupboard as I hear about encroaching power outages and blackouts looming. Out come flashlights, candles, matches and the two oil lamps, half full with wicks trimmed. Check my supply of water and emergency supplies. Will this be the time I will use the bag of "evacuee" clothes packed and ready in the closet? When I peer out the front door it bangs full open in the wind and lashing ice pellets and I remember the darkened parking lot, the tree without lights.

Uneasiness gives way to deep misgivings, like a premonition, as I realize that my neighbours' house, and all of the houses around it, must be without light and warmth. How long? I wonder. Over the years we have chatted in the parking lot, exchanged weather pleasantries and surface news but I don't have a phone number or even a last name. How then can I offer a bed, water and food without risking danger on pavements made glassy and treacherous in the violence of the storm?

Ice Storm 2: Toronto, December 23rd, In the Darkness of the Storm

There'd been so much snow and ice I hadn't been able to put a foot out the door and was feeling a little stir-crazy. I'd always driven around the city a few nights before Christmas to see the displays of lights in store windows and on neighbourhood streets. A friend who lives on a well-trafficked road, and whose car, sheltered in an underground parking space, needed no digging out, took up the challenge and picked me up. This year's drive turned out to be a scavenger hunt of discovering light in the unlikeliest of dark places.

The houses on the side streets are black, grey, or white ghosts floating in the shadows. Softly falling snow, the only light on the roads, quickly covers ruts on unshovelled walks. Occasionally our headlamps briefly pick out small forests of breathtaking beauty: ice gleams silver and gold on trees still standing, and on the tangled glitter of branches piled in every front yard, until we are blocked by a fallen tree, its jagged gash a yellow wound.

Two days since the ice storm and yet few houses have window candles flickering. There are no Hydro or fire trucks here. No one is outside. An eerie silence seeps through the night, our tires and the distant whine of an ambulance the only sounds. Where have people gone to take shelter? To find food? We turn back, slowly, carefully wind our shadowy way towards a main road. The first two we try are dark all the way as we creep south, no towering street lamps, no lights from the houses on street after street. And then! So brief we almost miss it, a sideways glimpse of Christmas gaiety pierces the gloom. We turn into the street, stop the car to admire strings of multicoloured lights threading a door and a few front yard trees in lonely welcome.

Turning west again, we drive through more blacked-out streets and abandoned houses until we come out onto the blazing lights of Yonge St. People walk purposefully. The ubiquitous "seasonal" music floats sporadically from busy stores; doors open and close on late shoppers. The coffee shops are full. It's as if nothing has happened. We seem to have moved from surreal, disconnected, dream-like, dark ghost towns to the impermanence of a garishly lit street scene for a stage set.

Halfway home we turn east to the Beach and are abruptly immersed in black again and a sense of recurring unreality; streets and houses an immediate dark presence, with tiny dots of snow the only light on the road, its whitened surface now pocked in charcoal as snow turns to freezing needles swirling 'round the car's headlights in the whipping wind.

Relief floods through me as the road straightens south and I see the familiar double strip of yellow and red lights that is Queen St.: slow-moving car headlamps, snow-dusted stop lights, store windows lit with the season's offerings never more welcome. The rumbling rattle of the Red Rocket trolley — may its colours never change — tells us there will be light for at least our single row of Queen St. houses as it makes its stolid way, apparently impervious to weather.

We are not. There is no companionable cup of tea tonight as my friend hurries for home through darkness to see if the light she left is no illusion, to see that there is still warmth. I sip my tea, still in the dark about my neighbours, and they of me.

Ice Storm 3: Toronto, Christmas Day, Daylight Revelations

Only as we make our way on Christmas afternoon to my daughter's for dinner does the true extent and likely duration of the ice storm's damage hit home. It had been a happy Christmas Eve. My son drove from Ottawa through the windswept roads and cold of the storm's aftermath and, to my great relief, made it by the afternoon of the 24th. Nail-biting time for me. His older son joined us; he is a dismayed refugee from his blacked-out apartment but we are delighted — with a twinge of guilt on my part at the unexpected pleasure of his company as he takes my other arm on the way to dinner in a neighbourhood restaurant.

As we three wander home in the cold and the blowing snow I am thrilled to be outside in a wonderful wintry night, something I cannot do safely any more, not quite squelching questions (their insistence familiar since World War II days) about our good luck in the midst of so much misery and fear. My grandson takes the guest room bed, his dad, the couch in the living room. We wake up next morning happily together, grateful to cook bacon and eggs and Christmas sticky buns. Is it so strange to be happy even as we know how wretched others are in their powered-out homes and street refuges?

Now, driving for the first time in daylight, we witness the devastation. Still snow-hung branches and even whole trees are littered everywhere, some piled to the side, some blocking roads. Downed hydro wires are encircled with yellow tape and warning signs. Amazingly, my daughter's tree-lined street still has power. Conscious of our immediate good fortune, and newly pricked by the bounty in all of our lives, we put that aside to enjoy our marvellously chaotic family get-together, joined this year by a grandchild's friend, her travel plans to a family Christmas aborted by disabled roads and airports.

Safely home that night, TV still out, the radio intones what is known of the damage. Power is restored to 75,000 of the three million people who lost power. Many people cooked their turkey or lamb on barbecues and hibachis, some inside or in garages and suffered the effects of toxic fumes. What were they thinking? There are warnings that some will live in the dark and cold for as long as a week, maybe more. A long simmering "How can this be?" bubbles to the surface — and stays there.

Heartsick, I hear that 20 percent of Toronto's tree canopy is destroyed and city works crews are hard-pressed to clear fallen trees and branches from hundreds and hundreds of streets — the buzz of wood chippers will fill the air for days.

Wearily I listen to arguments about the long-delayed necessity of burying power lines versus the cheaper popular choice. Or of how the city — "we" taxpayers — cannot afford arborists who know how to prune trees so that they can withstand heavy ice and wind — and save trees, and money, in the long run. Not until spring will we know the full damage to trees, the costs to repair huge potholes in the roads left by tarmac heaves, burst and aging water mains, people's homes and their disrupted lives, some changed forever.

Ice Storm 4: Toronto December 27, Reaching Out

Street nurse, Cathy Crowe, writes in the *Toronto Star* that City Council has no plan for the vulnerable, no plan to find and care for people living alone — cold and hungry, scared and suffering, some unable to leave dark homes for warm shelter and food.

When we let ourselves think about it we can understand the long-term consequences of depleted city tree canopies and increasingly imperiled infrastructure. But do we let ourselves think about who and where the vulnerable are — in our own cities and worldwide — in a few years' time? We seem to be moving backwards, not even at a standstill.

Can you imagine an earthquake like Tohoku strong enough to shift the earth on its axis between 10 and 25 cm? Or conceive the wretchedness of a people whose detritus still washes up on ocean shorelines? Twenty-two thousand dead and injured, many more homeless and never to return to their villages because of widespread, irreparable damage to the Fukushima Daiichi nuclear plant.

Tohoku, Katrina, Haiyan — cultural calamities whose names have already become metaphors for disaster. Named so we will remember? Or to distance us from the suffering and ravages wrought by tornadoes, typhoons, hugely destructive forest fires, desertification and drought, famine, garbaged oceans and plastic-rimmed shorelines that already threaten food sources for all living beings. Arctic sea ice is melting so fast that it may presage a new ice age.[1] The oldest association of earth scientists, the London Society, has designated our times a new geological era, the Anthropocene, a human-caused extinction event.

I feel as if so much gathered anger and sadness will burst me open. Years of accumulating knowledge and warnings, briefly come home to roost in the answers demanded by immediate dislocation and suffering, are soon blown away in "concerns" about money, "man" power, and priorities: how all levels of government "must cut costs, balance budgets ... until ..." Once more obfuscating the frightful question of how to "manage" catastrophic climate change — of how all living beings will live with the consequences.

I feel "lost and lonely" right now, as an old friend of mine said about so many elders who live alone, and worn-out too, as people who "go against the grain" can be. It's so easy to feel "overwhelmed and beyond our capacity" as Hydro officials said when frustrated customers jammed the call lines and prevented repaired lines from being powered on. We too lose sight of our power to effect change, fearful of losing the easier-living comforts we worked so hard for, or still aspire to. And in the midst of our harried lives it is hard to look beyond ourselves, or to even imagine that our small actions can make a difference.

Yet, somehow I "go on," as people astonishingly do. I hold on to the tenuous threads of companionable everyday life, the colours of hope, and muster my late-won Internet skills to reach out and join with those who must think what to do "in the meantime" as strength is summoned to keep on working in the now and for the future to lift the siege of our vulnerable, incredibly lonely, deep blue-green planet.

There is hope for a slow thaw. Too fast and the branches, laden with beauty's saving grace, will snap and fall to the ground, leaving wounds to heal in the cold and dark of a long winter (and worried questions about orchards and food in the spring).

To begin, I will learn the last names of my neighbours, I will plant another garden in spring. I will speak out a poem.

What the Ground Says

The green sweetness of sun on morning
mist drifts over a meadow, so different from
overcast early-day fog laden with fishy
reminders of lake water over grass.

What does the ground say when wetness pushes
through populated pavements? Through rush-hour
effluent? Thick factory plumes
with beckoning memories?

Every breath rhythms
whatever space is given.

ENDNOTES

---

[1]Elizabeth Kolbert, *The Sixth Extinction: An Unnatural History* (New York: Henry Holt and Co., 2014).

Fit for Survival

THE LEATHERBACK SEA TURTLE IS A SPECIES VIRTUALLY unchanged since they began swimming the world's oceans 110 million years ago in the time of the dinosaurs. Embodiment of the mysteries of survival and a cultural icon, they navigate the seas across thousands of kilometres of entire ocean basins, dive as deep as 4200 feet (1280 metres) for food, and can stay down for up to 85 minutes. The leatherback is so different from other marine turtle species that it is a taxonomic family of its own, called Dermochelyidae. The only remaining member of their original family, they are now critically endangered.

These wonderful creatures have survived for millennia because of a uniquely heavy, but leathery and flexible, inky-blue carapace that is ridged along the back, which protects them as well as giving them a more hydrodynamic structure. Leatherbacks have a very strong sense of smell and sight that can detect an enemy from a distance, and they can use claws against attack.

They propel themselves forwards with their front flippers in a swimming-like motion averaging close to 2.5 km per hour as they traverse the longest migration pattern between breeding and feeding areas of any sea turtle, averaging 3700 miles (6000 kilometres) each way.

Through an unusual set of adaptations they can maintain warm body temperatures in cold water and travel in tropical and temperate waters. But their transoceanic routes through Atlantic, Pacific and Indian Oceans and the Mediterranean Sea, as far north as Canada and Norway, and as far south as New Zealand and South America, are largely unknown. And where the hatchlings feed in the deep ocean is still a mystery.

Now they die in the thousands, thrown away as bycatch by the fishing industry and killed for oil, food, leather and jewelry. Developed coastlines eliminate habitat, changing sea temperatures impact hatchling sex ratios and species survival. Polluted oceans destroy the gelatinous zooplankton and other soft-bodied creatures, like salps, that are their food.

In a documentary, I watch the huge female (some grow to 1.8 metres and weigh as much as 680 kg) laboriously drag herself with her front flippers from the tropical ocean's edge to a safe nesting place in the same beach where she herself was hatched — the only time she will ever return to land. Sand flying through the air, she digs a body pit with her front flippers and then a smaller egg chamber with her back flippers where she will lay four to seven egg clutches of 50 to 90 billiard-ball-sized eggs over a month's time. She covers the nest with sand, packing it down with rear flippers, and then throws more sand around with her front flippers to help disguise the body cavity and nest. After the last clutch is laid she returns to her ocean home, but her telltale trail from nest to ocean is unmistakable.

Hatched en mass after 60 days the babies make a frantic multi-night rush to deep water, feeding on leftover egg yolk. One in a thousand from the hundreds of clutches laid in the sand survives predators from land, air and sea.

I see a mother begin her long journey back to her breeding grounds. She swims through a bay where fishermen have worked their gill nets for so many years the practice is like a myth — it is their heritage, change never considered. Her flippers can only propel her forward; she cannot reverse, is entangled in netting and cannot back out to save herself. Most die — eight a day in only one of many gill nets of many small fishermen in this small area. Thousands die in commercial operations.

In this small Trinidadian bay, marine biologists attach a satellite telemetry device on a female turtle's back so that migratory routes and habitat use can be identified, and ways to help them survive can be devised. The women and men of the team talk with the fishermen as they work with the turtles, explain what is happening to turtles worldwide, show them how best to free the enmeshed turtles and mend their nets, and discuss the possibility of other methods of fishing. They take their time.

I find her in myself; each of us embodies stories of survival. We humans haven't been around for nearly as long as leatherback turtles, but we share some durable characteristics. Turtles and humans have millennia of experience and learning. Each of us has a long history of strength and endurance, and now, the tension and mystery of balancing old and new ways of resourcefulness so that we can survive. Turtles have survived without us and our questions since before we inhabited the earth. Considering that in a few short years we have brought them, and perhaps ourselves, to the brink of extinction, is it really us they need now? Can this pattern be rewoven?

Turtles can no longer swim far enough or deep enough to escape from us. And they cannot swim backwards. Humans are the first predators that have made reversing an evolutionary necessity for them. Who knows how long, in the evolutionary scheme of things, this may take? They clearly don't have time to adapt to the conditions that threaten their survival now. Some of us, like the scientists I saw, hope that learning more about them will help them live in a world we now must share. Others are trying to help the turtles disentangle from the mess we unknowingly created for them in our search for food.

Observing the leatherback turtle's dilemma and our efforts to enable our co-existence I wonder, "Can humans learn to reverse course before we are inextricably entangled in a way of life that may lead to our extinction?" Not to go back to a Utopian way it was, but to move towards the largely and scarily unknowable way it could be?

It is said that we humans are the first species to realize how we impact our environment, ourselves, and other species worldwide. We have learned how to reach out to each other all over the world at lightning speed. What are we saying to each other that will begin the long task of disentangling us from the nets of destruction we have woven around ourselves? Can we, like the turtle hatchlings, dive deep into the mysterious places that feed us until we are able to offer a way forward?

I am a jumble of fascination and frustration, of despair enmeshed in a deep caring. I live with and try to truly understand the ways "we" misuse or ignore our knowledge from the past. Balancing my sadness, and a debilitating sense of defeat, is hope that we will piece together new learning and old knowledge to weave the unforeseeable future we must plan for as best we can:

We can reflect on the ways our elders have charted a course through centuries of turbulence to get us this far. We can be mindful of the nurturing mother-line reaching back millennia and feeding us forward. We must trust the passion, exuberance and love of our grandchildren.

Life Lines
Nature's Lineage

Marilyn Walsh, "Spring Song," Wings and Wires series, 2008, Mixed media, etchings with embroidery, 6 x 4 inches.

Tasting the Manitoulin

Just off the ferry. Two travel-weary people breathe in
the first taste of the Manitoulin. Sun-sharp, fish-laden —
filling mouths and lungs. Forty minutes to Mindemoya market.

Will there be early lettuce and spring onions left this late,
tucked among winter pickles, mustards,
new-baked bread and sticky buns? There will be smiles
of welcome, half-gloved hands to shake, Maya's salad
for a later lunch. Coffee warm in our bellies,
we roll down the dirt road to the cottage —
open doors, windows, sniff last year's fire,
see the still-swirling dust motes, smell the afterair
vinegar from the cottage cleaning. Look around
for changes before heading out to the herb patch.

Chives and mint are taking over — savoury, sage
and parsley just up. The rosemary and tarragon
have survived. Can these be seeded nasturtiums?
And lady's mantle? Salad burnet quivers beside the sorrel.
The lovage is pale and stunted; it must soon be moved.
Gathering salad herbs for buttered bread, we drag chairs
from the shed, stretch our faces to the sun, or —
wrapped in blankets — to a rain-specked windowpane.

No unpacking 'til the shower's passed, maybe longer —
why resist a nap? To dream of asparagus with lemon butter,
of strawberries that are almost heaven and Ted's

latest hybrid that worked; of Mary's buns and pies
with new flavours from Our Garden, six kinds of Norma's cookies
and honeycomb in little wooden crates.
Abundance lies ahead: Blue Jay Creek will weigh my lettuce,
invite me to an art show, Loon Song garden will have kale
and luscious weaving. J.D.'s will help me fill the garden gaps
with chervil, dill and red geraniums to brighten up the steps —
front and back. The list is long. I could go on
but it's time to head downhill to the dock. Inhale the tastes
of wind over lake water, toe test it for a swim,
so another summer can begin.

Manitoulin Laundry Lines

Summers, I write encircled in the magic
of Manitoulin Island — wet days, washing machines whirl
in the communal laundry room.

Neighbours forecast the day — go fishing or read a book?
In fair weather, lake winds buffet jeans and T's on a line
strung from tree to tree, flap child-memories

of "a good drying day" as the last sock is hung.
Heels turn out, toes face each other on the days
when writing is stuck. Go for a swim,

stretch out on the dock — remembering ideas
hanging out across my Lake Mindemoya cottage
before wireless, or any kind of hook-up.

Lines of recipe cards in orderly queues
string the room from window frame to curtain rod.
Awash in images, ideas swish back and forth,

spill over to other cards, change places,
shift chapters. Thoughts billow. The lines crowd.
More and more cards dangle, jostle for a dry-run,

stretch out, fill a book that recalls —

post-workshop dirty work
my favourite laundry line of all.

Not sheets or clothes or socks but 16 sponges:
pink, yellow, green and blue, each pinned
between cedar and maples, fade in the sun and wind

as they dry into hard little oblongs after a day
of paint and clay. Their chemical origins betrayed,
even as they hold remnants of form and colour

and the makings of memories.

Forecast

I wake to the long sigh of the mourning dove.
Sink within her silences. Eyes open
to leaf patterns on the wood floor
shifting to forecast which way
the wind will blow.

Tomorrow leaf shadows may dance wildly, or not
appear at all. Rain sounds fill the emptiness
of no bird call or sun-made tracery, reminding me
to listen for the spaces in loneliness
I too quickly move to fill.

Lake Escape

The morning lake scape ripples crossways to shore,
first light quivers in a southeast breeze. A duck swims by
in a hurrywhere? A gull, one-legged on the dock post,
takes off. I fly with her

low over green island fingers strung across the foreground,
higher over the encircling mainland arms stretched behind them
like the road going 'round to town between land-lines of gold —
flowering canola, undulating wheat fields, corn stalks silken
   heavy.

Farther, to flat grey alvar granite, tiny pitted pools teem
with life invisible to us. Wandering cracks hold rare orchids,
creeping juniper, fauna fossils that lived 400 million years ago
and hundred-year growths of bracken in slow inching curves.

Set down on the edge of vastness, the Huron's "Great Big Sea."
Whimbrels and peregrine falcons pull memories of why
there is a Misery Bay — sunken lake boats, early settlers starving
until they meet land the Native way. Knowledge lives dry now

under hard grey roads strung out over sacred places.
Night lights on either side of the lake reach out
to ink-black islands, glimmer around houses. A slow beckon
to the quiet grunt of dark water on stone and wet boards.

Shore Reeds

A loon calls clear
across the lake, pulls me
from bed to boat in minutes.

Coffee and bun balanced
between boat ribs,
I ease away from the dock

leave as little notice
on the water
as the loon's quick dive.

I hug the near shore towards
the marsh, whisper-scrape
through thin shore reeds

glistening with night dew,
alert for the rightful inhabitants.
Reeds so tall my eye levels

with tiny, bulging galls
along their green length.
Reeds so dense I can eat

breakfast as the minnows do,
paddle-fin steadying me
in the imperceptible current,

listen to frog gulps, feel a thrust
of air — a sandpiper signals,
I'm not good company.

I watch lacy water-weeds
sway, skate bugs quick-stepping
among them feeding, and food.

Lily buds unfurl before
my eyes. The warming
sun spurs opening.

A fresh breeze stirs my hair,
nudge-rocks the canoe, shifts
the reeds to disturb a resting fish.

Her swift departure alerts
two Blanding's turtles. Immobile
on matching lily pads, they raise

matching eye folds, let me
know I am not so well disguised.
An intruder

in their waking world, I
push off, a paddle tip's slight swirl
bubbling the thick muck below,

rustle-click my way through
their brightening reed forest.
The lifting mist transforms us

all from modest pastels to shining
noisy colours moving in rhythm
to the new morning.

Foreplay

How many ways does the wind touch,
curl a sleeve, lift a collar, pucker
skin, disturb a strand of hair?

I unbutton
slow-slip off my clothes,
prolonging the anticipation.

Beckoned to the water's edge,
I step down
slide into her cool embrace.

Wind and water
play with me. I roll over, face
to the moon and stars.

Skinny Dip

Star shapes on the water
floating by reflect creatures
invisible to human eyes.

Naked on the edge of the dock
I watch the sun slant through
the orange lichened rocks

down to the bottom of the zebra
musselled lake. No minnows dart up
for food — there's nothing left to take.

Even so, my muscles sigh as the sun
dries my skin, eyes closing to reveal
the small bestowed radiance within.

The World Is Young

Tender almost-green unfurlings
top the tallest, oldest trees.

Moist dark tendrils show the first
purple of painted Japanese fern

sheltered under white-edged
hosta and shiny holly leaves.

Creamy Solomon's seal bells
hang over the striped hood

of a new jack-in-the-pulpit
four feet from last year's spot —

a squirrel nipped the top from
its parent, now exposed without

her hood. How will she grow
in summer's heat?

Morning Rain

Gulls clatter on the roof
gorging on shad flies, the rest
live out their day-long lives
       on sunny morning walls.

Hummingbirds dart back and forth
at the feeder — Sip-look, sip-look,
always look, looking
Mostly they fight each other.

Six ducklings hurry in a tight line behind
       their mother —
Her DNA instructs this camouflage.
Yesterday there were seven.

The early sun warms my goosebump skin,
through a sweater, leaves shiver,
       my eyes shift
to dark-bottomed clouds moving fast

over the horizon. Milk skims on cooling coffee.
Spellbound I wait — diagonal grey streaks join
      water and sky,
race across the lake.

Daisy and goldenrod stems bend, cedar berries
clack, bird sounds stop, paper flips,
      the pen rolls.
My skin chills as the first drops needle my face.

Summer Carpet

Clover frosts the grass,
scattered rosy leaves
weave a carpet with golden butter and eggs,
guide the daisies and rusty Indian
paintbrush through the shrubby backdrop.
Bees move and hum,
become fat before my eyes.

Twenty-four Hours

Last night in the big wooden chair I watched
bats come out as darkness crept along the shore,
blackened the trees to leafless silhouettes on indigo.

This morning I leave my bed at seven to sit at the picnic table,
shed my dressing gown, then flannel shirt. The sun climbs
the trees to wind-shimmer on water and turned up leaves.

The first white clouds of an autumn day drift up
over the treed horizon, sneak overhead as I write.
Move a table under the trees at noon.

Pale grey leaf shadows quiver on a sunny patch of grass.
A book, a comfortable lunch. The birds quiet down
with me to doze in cedar shade. Tai Chi on the dock,

a late afternoon swim with the duck family. Is that a leech?
Scoop it away, recalling how a small granddaughter clutches
my neck, submerges us. We bob up laughing — she almost shrieks.

Precious wet skin warmth, her chatter at supper, sleepover
stories at night, burrowing under bed covers in the morning.
The riot of sunset deepens and the lake gleams pink

through rust red sumac and goldenrod. This time last week
the stutter of her motorbike as she chugged down the lake
after Sunday dinner.

The Fox Islands*

Sails furled, passengers dive off the boat and swim to shore.
We — Margaret and I — stand on the deck, smile, nod,
pretend it's fine.
                              He comes
'round the stern mooring line in the yellow towed zodiac
"Come on, I'll take you over," hands us in, rows to a shallow

landing. Shoeless we wade ashore, climb on huge round
layered rocks the colour of pink roses unfolding, step
over small pools, hunker down, watch minute creatures swim

in their sea. Our eyes drift over stubby evergreens to thin silver
grasses creviced in dark creases to the pale bent horizon. We
stretch out, arms and legs flung wide cradled in warm stone

ravished by smooth silky folds of roseate granite old as time.

*Near Killarney, on the north shore of Georgian Bay.

Cover-up

Last night's fog
drifts through trees and meadow grass,
pearls see-through morning cobwebs

The first breeze
shifts dark green shadows from the far shore
closer with each slow ripple

Fish snaps
disturb the surface. The ducks wait. The mist
lifts as the light slants through

I'm with the ducks.
alert for the dip of an early morning paddle
as water bubbles fur my skin.

Need I care for other than lake cover
to caress my glistening
folds?

Staying Warm in Winter

DOCK

As soon as the ground is dry enough Dave drives the Case Tractor over to the meadow at cottage #9 — drags the dock down to the water. He looks for what is left of the underwater path and seats the dock on rocks as close to them as he can. He bolts the steps fast to the left side and weighs them down with more rocks. Water surges and races; accommodating this new peninsula, washes water around the worn wintered-over boards.

The boards are laid horizontally in a vertical frame, flanked at the end on either side by old rusted hay-wagon wheels that stabilize the dock — it lends a certain Ferris wheel gaiety. Weathered a dozen shades of grey-brown, lichen-splotched grey-green with occasional patches of white, yellow and orange — like daubs of paint, some of the boards must be nailed down again. Loosened by snow and ice.

STONES AND PATH

The dock is set down on stones, anchored by stones, surrounded by stones. Each year it comes to rest in a different place because the waves and the ice have moved the stones around — there seem to be more big ones every year. Each year, as soon as possible, we remake the underwater path through the stones, and past the end of the dock to a place deep enough to swim in. My daughter Meg has the stronger back and braves the icy spring lake so cold that she feels her legs go numb in minutes and must lie on the dock boards to warm up before wading back into the water. Every year we know we're lucky when the sun shines on us at least one day on opening weekend. This year the path angles more sharply away from the edge of the dock. There is no handhold at the end and I must find small spaces in between those immovable boulders where a foot can find a steady pause on the way to the deeper water — essential for the many stormy days when gloriously crashing waves can easily throw me off balance.

Wearing sunglasses and a peaked cap, I carry a stick in my right hand so I don't slip going down the slope to the lake, especially after a rain, or in the morning when the grass is still wet. A towel and swim shoes in my left hand and a noodle for balance thrown over my shoulder, I walk down to the four-plank bridge over the stones to the dock.

I step carefully on wobbly planks toward wooden steps on the left side. I place my stick and the noodle behind a towel so they won't roll into the water. I put my left foot on the first step and then my right one on the second, grab the handrail as the steps bounce with my weight — heaving a little when the waves are high — and say another thank you to Doug Alkenbrach and John Bouie for building the possibility of swimming.

WATER AND STONES

In high summer the lake is still and flat — the mirrored boards underneath the dock are a dark, mythical twin, stirring with the movement of water and my footsteps above. Cooling-off swims are long and lazy. I slowly float out to forever — gently kick back to shore and dock. The big rocks are more than stumbling stones, they are welcome places to sit along the way when the waves make it hard for me to stand up and reach the end of the dock. Sometimes I perch on the bottom step and watch the water seethe over stones, changing their colour with each surge. Depending on the time of day and the slant of the sun — on and off, on and off, like a lighthouse beacon — white foam eddies around bared rock tips, rising up like small islands.

Close to the grassy shore, covered with the advancing seasons' wildflowers — butter and eggs, yellow-centred daisies, purple vetch, Queen Anne's lace, red and yellow devil's paintbrush, goldenrod — the waves swell or swish back and forth to meet the shoreline rocks: dry/shiny, dry/shiny, languid, rippling the fronded sedges at lake's edge. Even on clear-as-glass days, when the water barely moves, I can hear a quiet hiss, or small murmurs of shifting pebbles.

Minnows and tiny gobies dart around between the nearshore stones, seek shaded protection under the dock. There are fewer now. The ugly, black zebra mussels clumped tight to the rocks have cleared the water of minnow food and our food too. What power! Having their way with us from the bottom of the food chain to the top.

Ducks like docks and shallow water too. They swim under the dock when no one is on it, pick up speed and swim quickly past when I am sitting. When I am swimming, they circle way around me or turn back and wait for me to leave, sometimes arching out of the water, or taking momentary flight, showing me what they want me to do. Sunlit drops of water fly from their speckled wings.

BEING THERE

Lying on the dock, full length and face down; I wiggle and shift to find woody places among the boards that don't dig into flesh, leave splinters. I watch the water under the dock, listen mesmerized by ceaseless gurgling swishes. I become the lazy movement over water. Then roll over slowly so I do not to hurt a rib. I've done that and been bruised for weeks. Let the sun dry my skin and bathing suit. Early mornings I lie naked, savouring the first heat in every skin fold and crease, softened muscles melting into the warming dock boards one by one.

I pull my hat down enough to shade my eyes and still watch the gulls wheeling overhead. They swoop down to reclaim their place at the end of the dock, carrying crabs to crack open. They veer away when I bang a shoe on the boards or pitch small stones to stop them from pooping in the water; they squall in protest.

Late summer morning wake-up swims are hasty and vigorous until the water gets too cold, even for that. Wrapped in the largest towel I dry my hair in the wind or dangle my feet over the edge in the last of the afternoon sun, splashing into memories.

Finally, it's time for a chair in the sun at the end of the dock, leaving the autumn-shaded meadow to read or gaze over the lake towards Treasure Island and watch lights begin to glow over Mindemoya shore.

Soon crinkled brown leaves swirl down onto the dock and catch themselves in the cracks between boards. They make a mouldering, knobby surface. Leaves float on the water then huddle back to shore — premonition of snow to come.

The dock is pulled out of the lake so it won't heave with winter ice and then be yanked away by rolling next spring waves to float down the shoreline to who knows where.

In winter, the dock rests on the meadow near shore. There it stays, slowly becoming heaped with drifts of snow and ice — a bulge in the landscape holding separation and remembrance.

Last Day

Hunker down on the leeward deck
outside the boat house
lean against the old car rug, ready
for cloud-cover chill, last day
to listen to water run under boards
smell new pine needles
pick a yellow cluster of cedar berries
for medicine, with a sweetgrass braid
and a few shreds of tobacco
to ward off city spells.

Twilight

A different quiet
than midday's torpid blaze
when even the ants are idle
      and no leaf stirs.

Black cut-out trees
fixed against navy-blue sky,
      a Sunset lake,
Swimmers leave no golden wake.

It Shouldn't Feel Like Dying

A flock of geese circles the lake crying
"*One last look?*" as I do, in stages,
these last September days.

Goldenrod heads turned lacy brown
sprout pink caterpillar plumes. Blood-red sumac
fruit along the shore scavenged for Christmas jelly.

Green tomatoes linger, squash hides under cardboard,
onions and too many zucchini wait on the back steps
for the relish kettle.

Rusty-edged geranium leaves, sparse blossoms
stretched on spindly stems — take a cutting.
Last trim for the grass. Time for Meeker's Mix.

Sun on the lake reflects cool diamonds. Stiff
rustling yellow leaves drift down, forecast
woodsmoke, a soup pot simmering
for a twilight supper.

Appendix

WEAVE & MEND

Songwriter: Mary Trup

Old woman is watching, watching over you
In the darkness of the storm, she is watching
She is weaving, mending, gathering the colours
She is watching over you.

> *Chorus*
> So weave and mend
> Gather the fragments safe
> And win the sacred circle sisters
> Weave and mend, weave and mend,
> Oh women, weave and mend.

Old woman is weaving, gathering the threads
Her bones become the loom she is weaving,
She is watching, weaving, gathering the colours
She is watching over you.

> *Chorus*
> For years I've been watching, waiting for old woman
> Feeling lost and so alone, I've been watching.
> Now I find her weaving, gathering the colours
> Now I find her in myself.

Acknowledgements

I am so grateful to the many generous people who gave their time and energy to help bring this book to fruition. My heartfelt thanks to Michael Salter and Anne Champagne for wise and patient editorial advice, to Anne for endless hours of copy editing, and to Claire Kathleen Grandy, Sonia Di Placido, Gianna Patriarca, Donna Langevin, John Parry, Isobel Harry and Allan Briesmaster for generous hours of editorial assistance.

Marilyn Walsh's unique images for the chapter headings add the much-appreciated *je ne sais quoi* that enlivens pages of printed text.

Kudos to Margaret Lam and Emily Wood for ultra-professional web design and maintenance and for creating an online presence for *Laundry Lines: A Memoir in Stories and Poems* and its author. Emily's concept for the cover is both enticing and whimsical.

Harriet Kideckel provided a wonderful portrait for the book and for publicity and I am grateful for the time and energy that Alex Broughton and Peter Nelson gave for the book trailer.

It's difficult to say enough about the unqualified support offered by Mary Shirley-Thompson, Marilyn Luciano, Ellen Ryan and Mairy Beam. Many thanks for putting up with me during the ups and downs of writing and production.

And of course thanks to Luciana Ricciutelli, wise and kind editor, who opened a space to welcome *Laundry Lines: A Memoir in Stories and Poems* to the Inanna family, and to Renée Knapp for helping to cast the lines far and wide.

Epigraphs:

Jeanne Perreault, *Writing Selves: Contemporary Feminist Autography* (Minneaplosi, MN: University of Minneapolis Press, 1995), p. 133, quoted by Nancy Viva Davis Halifax in "There is More to be Done" in Chapter 11 of *The Art of Poetic Inquiry*, ed. S. Thomas, A. Cole and S. Stewart (Big Tancook Island, NS: Backalong Books, 2012).

Jodi Picoult, *The Storyteller* (New York: Emily Bestler Books/ Washington Square Press, 2013).

Kelley Aitken, "Why Visual Art?" in *The Art of Poetic Inquiry,* ed. S. Thomas, A. Cole and S. Stewart (Big Tancook Island, NS: Backalong Books, 2012), p. 67.

About Marilyn Walsh:

Art has always been a part of my life. I was born in Quebec, the sixth generation of my family in Canada. I grew up surrounded by grandmothers, aunts, and a mother who created comfort and magic out of scraps of cloth and thread. They taught me how to embroider. I wish to honour that heritage and the natural beauty of Canadian birds throughout the year.

In 2008, I graduated from the three-year Adult Art Program at Central Technical School in Toronto. There I was introduced to a wide range of artistic practise: sculpture, printmaking, painting, photography, ceramics, drawing, and design.

Even though hanging out our wash in all the seasons was hard work, I loved the sweet scent of bringing in the sun and wind-dried laundry. Now, as more people become more energy and ecology oriented, they are becoming interested in these "solar drying devices."

The embroidery thread brings energy to these pastoral scenes. There are invisible threads tying us to our home, to our place in the landscape. Those threads tug at our insides when we return to our birthplace.

Visit my website at marilynwalsh.com.

Photo: Harriet Kideckel

Ann Elizabeth Carson, writer, poet, artist, was honoured as one of Toronto's Mille Femme at the 2008 Luminato Festival for her contribution to the arts. Ann writes and sculpts full-time in Toronto and on Manitoulin Island, reads at multimedia events, and leads workshops in the arts. Previously a counsellor and instructor at York University, and a recently retired psychotherapist, Ann has devoted her career to understanding the silenced voices in our society and attempting to give them voices in her writing. Her work has appeared in numerous journals, magazines, and anthologies, and in four published books.